Charismania

'Roland Howard's investigation into the weaknesses of the Charismatic Renewal is characteristically hard hitting, making sober reading. The book will appeal to many who are concerned about the growth, fragmentation and trajectory of recent charismatic phenomena.'

— *Martyn Percy*

Charismania

When Christian Fundamentalism Goes Wrong

Roland Howard

Mowbray
A Cassell Imprint
Wellington House
125 Strand
London WC2R 0BB

PO Box 605
Herndon
VA 20172

First published 1997

British Library Cataloguing-in-Publication Data
A catalogue record for this book is available from the British Library

ISBN   0-264-67409-X

Typeset by Stephen Wright, The Rainwater Consultancy, Longworth, Oxfordshire

Printed and bound in Great Britain by Biddles Limited, Guildford and King's Lynn

Contents

Introduction

As we approach the millennium there is an increasing sense that such an apparently significant date must be the harbinger of good or ill. Prophecies, ancient and modern, promising heaven or hell, cling to the date like a desperate swimmer to a lifeline. Cults, gurus, clerics and prophets predict the end of the world or a utopian new age, with an unnerving certainty that is clearly increasingly attractive to people in search of security. New religious movements (or, in the words of their critics, cults) and extreme interpretations of mainstream religions are experiencing something of a revival. This pre-millennial tension is not unprecedented. The period leading up to the first millennium was also a time of great uncertainty and expectancy. Several religious groups waited for midnight, anticipating rapture (the end of the world), and were bemused to look up and realize that it was business as usual.

Ironically, a thousand years later in a largely secular, hi-tech, educated society, the very things that symbolize our progress appear to be pointing us back towards a desire for certainty and security and the idea of a benign God becomes increasingly attractive. Even in this post-Glasnost world, the people at the tail-end of the twentieth century live with the knowledge that, however unlikely, destroying the planet with nuclear weapons is possible. We are told that in geological time the human race has only existed for the less than a second in an hour; and yet modern, pollution belching consumerism makes another thousand years seem distinctly unlikely. Rain forests fall, global warming continues, the hole in the ozone spreads and no one nation, institution or leader appears to have the authority or ability to take the long term view and call a stop to it. Add to this the oft-quoted fact that the twentieth century has seen more killed in war than all the preceding centuries in human civilization put together, and the notion that the irrevocable march of scientific progress and enlightened democratic capitalism is not quite what it is cracked up to be, gains credibility.

The uncertainty (some might say chaos) of current social, political and environmental reality adds an intensity to the quest for security which may well be greater than that felt during the dark age of the tenth century. Is it any wonder that people are seeking security in otherworldly spiritual solutions? Is it any wonder that leading people to such security is (among other things) a lucrative growth industry? For the western world-weary pilgrim there are two principal routes to spiritual security: the eclectic range of New Age beliefs or Charismatic Christianity.

New Agers and Charismatics are both experiencing revival in the UK, the USA and in Western Europe. It seems no coincidence that both groups exhibit a retreat from rationality and a desire to experience the supernatural, the 'magical', in everyday life. Sectors of both groups have also made grandiose claims about 'imminent', supernatural changes (or intervention) to civilization. The surrounding chaos and what has been called Pre-Millennial Tension (PMT) may have led to these groups expanding and, not surprisingly, the groups themselves appear to be more deeply affected by this tension than most.

Although New Age beliefs may be as popular as those of Charismatic Christians because of the individualistic and idiosyncratic nature (and vastly different beliefs) of most New Age groups, Charismatic Christianity may legitimately be described as the largest unified religious movement experiencing rapid growth in the UK. Apart from any spiritual gains, it offers adherents a friendly, secure and supportive community. At its best it has offered help to the poor and disadvantaged, has sought to challenge racism and inequality, and has shown compassion to AIDS victims and the terminally ill. Many would say that it has much to offer society.

However, in recent years, certain obscure and unorthodox doctrines have spread that seem to have led to families splitting, mental illness, sexual abuse, suicide attempts and deaths. The growth of these doctrines has been such that they have entered mainstream Charismatic belief and threaten to hijack the whole movement. Spiritual warfare is a doctrine, in the view of its protagonists, whose time has come. Its critics see it as a dangerous, paranoid delusion which is as unchristian as it is damaging. Its potential for abuse is almost limitless.

In essence the doctrine of spiritual warfare is the belief that we are surrounded by demons and Satanic powers that we must defeat before we can live successful Christian lives. The demons or evil spirits may inhabit buildings, institutions, geographical areas, objects or people but wherever they are, they are met by Christians with a tremendous desire to fight them. The origins of spiritual warfare are found in the Bible in Paul's letters to the early church. They constitute a handful of verses which are somewhat sketchy and in no way outline (or were intended to outline) a comprehensive theology.

The writer of the letter to the Ephesians says that 'our battle is not against flesh and blood, but against the rulers, against the authorities, against the powers of this dark world and against the spiritual forces of evil in the heavenly realms.' He gives no clue about what he means by 'spiritual forces' but the general message of the letter is a plea for Christian unity. In his second letter to the Corinthians, Paul explains that Christians should not fight (by which he means argue or oppose) using the same weapons as non-Christians. In the context, the most obvious interpretation of this is that Christians should not get bogged down in complex point scoring debates but state what he saw as simple Christian truth instead.

What is most interesting about these verses is the significance that has been attached to them. They form a minuscule, slightly puzzling aspect of the canon of scripture, yet have attracted an amazing amount of interest in recent years. Scores of books have been written about spiritual warfare, organizations and events involving hundreds of thousands of people have been centred on it. Ask any Charismatic Christian about spiritual warfare and they will have a clear concept of what it is although compared with Christian teaching in the Bible about poverty, love or injustice it fades into insignificance. It seems quite possible that, in the countdown to the millennium, modern Charismatic Christians in their obsession with spiritual warfare are seeing what they want to see.

This is not to say that the concept of spiritual warfare is completely new. Christianity is historically in opposition to certain things in the 'world'. In essence (if not always in practice) it is not a passive religion: it opposes injustice, greed, sexual licence, abuse of power. Christianity believes good and evil are in opposition to each other (rather than in some way complementary) and stresses redemption in personal, social and economic terms. Traditionally spiritual warfare was a much more sedate affair which meant little more than that Christians were opposed to evil and that they should pray and act against it. Even those Christians who saw the devil as a literal being with a personality were more interested in opposing evil (whether in the shape of injustice, temptation, or deception) and bringing people into the faith, than battling it out with demons.

Charismatic Christians have other weapons in their arsenal. Alongside the doctrine of spiritual warfare they have the recently rediscovered 'spiritual gifts' such as healing, prophecy and exorcism. The rise of the Charismatic movement in the 1960s and 1970s, which was distinguished by these 'gifts', gave Christians supernatural (or 'magical') weapons with which to fight the devil. The use of these gifts was often seen as a combative fight with the forces of darkness. The more detailed doctrine of spiritual warfare (claiming that Christian prayer warriors are in constant combat with the 'spiritual powers in the heavenlies' which can alter the political, social, economic and spiritual realities on earth) is largely a development of the late 1980s onwards. Taken together it is clear that many Charismatic Christians are on the warpath. Indeed anything which appears to oppose (or raise questions about) Christianity has been interpreted as Satanic.

Some commentators have suggested that extreme religious concepts and practices (for instance, spiritual warfare and the intense concentration on supernatural/magical gifts) become pronounced when particular sects have been reacting against a dominant and threatening mainstream culture (puritanical Christians for example, in the New World). Interestingly this reaction to mainstream culture is what most sociologists use to distinguish between fundamentalism and 'traditional' Christianity: traditional Christians are those who do not react but continue in their beliefs, untroubled by the dominant culture; fundamentalists react strongly and tend to go on the offensive against what they perceive as evil, deceptive or dangerous mainstream culture. In sociological terms (and popular understanding) Charismatics are fundamentalists. (Theologically, one can say that Charismatics resemble fundamentalists, but that the emphasis on the fundamental inerrancy of the Bible has been fused with, or superseded by, the inerrancy of Charismatic experience).

Introduction

The intention of this book is to describe and consider the sinister consequences of spiritual warfare and what some have called 'Christian magic' for the church and wider society. Formerly Christians believed that they were struggling with the world, the flesh and the devil, but these days emphasis on the complex grey areas (such as the personality and senses) has been dropped in favour of that unambiguous object of hate: the devil. Indeed, the devil is seen as Lord (or Prince) of the world. The imagination and energy of many (but not all) Charismatics has gone into increasingly arcane, subjective and superstitious methods of vanquishing the devil and his demonic sidekicks. Indeed, some of the practitioners of the 'Charismatic gifts' described in this book, appear to mirror the Satanic practices that they abhor.

The book is in three parts. The first section is a brief history of the Charismatic movement which charts the rise of the Charismatic gifts and spiritual warfare. The second section is a series of true stories showing the damaging effects of these practices on individuals. Finally the book examines the trends within the movement and how it fits into a wider cultural context. I want to make it clear that there are areas of the Charismatic church that are largely free from the phenomena that this book describes. There are many compassionate and sensitive Charismatic churches working with the weak and disadvantaged. It is the nature of this book that it will highlight the extremes rather than the norm but my central argument is that the extremes are fast becoming the norm and that this will have dangerous consequences. It is also true that if extreme beliefs and practices have certain key characteristics in common (for instance, a fascination with power, a ferocious desire to fight 'evil' and a highly subjective, supernatural emphasis) then they become signposts, or warning signs, about the direction of the movement. This book raises big questions about the Charismatic church and its practices and it is my genuine hope that Charismatics will read and consider the contents. Indeed, if they do so, it will prove that the picture I have painted is too bleak.

The Origins of the Charismatic Movement in the UK

The beginnings of the Charismatic movement, as any good Charismatic will tell you, are in the New Testament. Whatever one's view of the Bible, there is no getting round the fact that the Gospels and the Acts of the Apostles and many of Paul's letters to the early church bear witness to miraculous happenings. The New Testament describes miraculous healings, prophecies, exorcisms, as well as show-stopping feats of catering, brewing and climatic intervention – not to mention the heart of the Christian faith, the Resurrection. Contrary to the view of some, Charismatic gifts did not start in a Revivalist tent of some quack preacher in the North American Bible belt.

In fact, accounts of the lives of the church fathers are equally clear in their descriptions of apparently miraculous events during the first few centuries of the Christian church. Descriptions of them petered out with time and by the time of Augustine in the fourth century they were all but non-existent. Augustine himself taught that the gift of speaking in tongues had been superseded by Christian love. For the Roman Catholic Church, miracle-working was not the norm; it was the territory of Saints. A few modern Protestant writers have argued that from the church fathers until the present day isolated groups or an underground church were practising the charismata (the spiritual gifts such as prophecy, healing, exorcism and speaking in tongues), but almost all scholars conclude that there is no evidence to back this up.

From about the fifth century until the early twentieth century, miracles (in the unequivocal New Testament sense) have not played a large part in traditional Christian theology or practice. The spiritual gifts were considered to have been given by God to the early Christians as a sort of kickstart to get the church on the road – despite medieval superstitions in the healing powers of relics of the Saints. Christian doctrine was considered to be the most important thing and faith became more closely aligned to tradition and to state. That is not to say that the church (largely in the form of religious orders operating under the authority of the Catholic Church) did not have much to offer society in helping the poor, in education and spreading Christianity. It is hard to imagine the modern church having the same effect on contemporary Britain as, for instance, the Benedictine monasteries had during the first millennium.

Christendom and Christian practice was largely a miracle-free zone until much more recently. Despite sporadic descriptions of charismata in the nineteenth century (most notably in a small sect called the Catholic Apostolic Church), there was little practice of the spiritual gifts. The Catholic Apostolic Church and the Brethren (another non-conformist sect) were interested to see whether the Holy Spirit (and attendant spiritual gifts) would be restored to the church in what they saw as 'the last days'. The Brethren ultimately rejected the possibility while Edward Irving and the Catholic Apostolics embraced it and, indeed, practised it, in the form of speaking in tongues and praying for miraculous healings.

However, it was about seventy years later when manifestations of the Holy Spirit really took off. In 1906, Pastor William Seymour began to hold services in an abandoned warehouse on Asuza Street, Los Angeles. He was an enthusiastic black pastor with a remarkably multi-ethnic congregation. During his services there were dramatic manifestations of the Charismatic gifts. Reports of speaking in tongues, miraculous healings and people converted as the Holy Spirit 'fell on them' as they entered the church, spread across the USA and into Europe.

According to Dr Meic Pearse, Lecturer in Church History at London Bible College, the situation was ripe for the birth of Pentecostalism. The emphasis on holiness and the belief in 'entire sanctification' (or being made sinless and completely holy) which had started centuries earlier with Wesley and the Methodists had developed into the belief that this happened with baptism in the Holy Spirit.

In the USA (a country whose Christian history is characterized by waves of revival) what is known as the Second Great Awakening (1800–30) involved, in some sectors, prophecy and speaking in tongues alongside an emphasis on personal holiness. This was a precursor of Pentecostalism in the twentieth century. Dr Pearse says: 'There was a great emphasis on using the power of God to become sanctified and serve others and, of course, this fitted in perfectly with the manifestations of the charismata.'

This movement which believed that it was rediscovering the Holy Spirit was called the Pentecostal movement after the first outpouring of the Holy Spirit at Pentecost, as described in the Acts of the Apostles. Seymour and Charles Parham, a minister working in Illinois, were probably the initiators but it is clear that the Americans were equally encouraged by the large numbers of converts in the Welsh revival. It was two way traffic in terms of encouragement but the manifestation of charismata started in Asuza Street. A year later, word of mouth, letter and pamphlet had taken it in to the Welsh valleys and to the Anglican Church of All Saints, Sunderland, whose minister was the Revd Alexander Boddy. At this stage 'pentecostal' was a term describing someone who experienced Charismatic gifts; it was not yet a denomination.

All Saints Church became a centre for those interested in baptism in the Holy Spirit at the beginning of the century. The Welsh revival spawned the Apostolic Church and the founders of the UK's other two Pentecostal congregations (Elim and the Assemblies of God) were also converted during the Welsh Revival. By the 1920s these three separate pentecostal denominations had been founded in the UK, forebears of the Charismatic revival which was to start forty years later simultaneously (some would say symbiotically) in the USA and the UK and spread at phenomenal speed around the world. Dr Meic Pearse says: 'Whatever one thinks of it and however one understands it, the Charismatic Church appears to be the future of Christendom. It is the only sector of the church growing in the UK and it is experiencing something akin to revival in Africa, southeast Asia and South America.'

Before describing the origins of the Charismatic movement in the UK it is worth saying a few words about the development of Pentecostal beliefs and the growth of tele-evangelism or what was later to become the 'electronic church' in the USA. By 1914 various independent pentecostal groups came together to form the Assemblies of God. Although nineteenth-century evangelicals were deeply committed to liberal preoccupations such as the emancipation of slaves, by the twentieth they were far more conservative in their outlook. Probably threatened by what they saw as an ungodly world, many retreated from social reform programmes and into fundamentalist interests such as the end of the world.

Fundamentalists had a more dogmatic interpretation of the Bible, clearer (and usually more lurid) beliefs about the end of the world, as well as stronger nationalism. It was fundamentalists who would describe the Soviet Union as the anti-Christ, due to appear shortly before the end of the world. Many fundamentalists supplied names of suspected communists to the House Committee of un-American activities during the McCarthy trials in the early 1950s. Fundamentalists would have nothing to do with what they called 'apostates' (Christians with a different theology) or with non-Christians. They separated themselves from the world partly because of 'holiness teaching' which gave them a desire to be pure, and partly because of what they saw as a decaying and depraved culture around them.

Indeed the term 'the world' or 'worldly' was increasingly used pejoratively to mean fallen, sinful or even devilish. Not surprisingly, fundamentalists reacted strongly against the emergence of youth culture. The devil's music (rock and roll and subsequently rock music) may initially have set young people alight, but on conversion they frequently set their record collections alight. When John Lennon provocatively claimed that The Beatles were 'bigger than Jesus' he had no idea that his comment would catalyze fundamentalist protest marches and record burnings across the country. Contact with 'the world' was increasingly seen as contamination while a rigid 'us and them' (saved and unsaved) dualism came into being.

Gradually a ghetto culture emerged and naturally a multi-million pound industry grew around this captive market. Quite apart from Christian books and music, a commercial subculture developed in which virtually all products and services could be provided by Christians. From diaries to deodorant, T-shirts to tea bags (with Bible verses attached), an outlook was developing in which things were not kosher if they were not Christian. The most significant aspect of this was the rise of Christian television.

Owing to a laissez faire regulation system, fundamentalists were able to buy airtime on TV networks. This started as filling Sunday morning slots and developed into wholly 'Christian' channels providing a mixture of twee family entertainment programmes and religious chat shows, healing services and mass rallies. Audiences were presented with emotionally frenzied meetings, supposed healings and other apparent manifestations of the Holy Spirit such as people being 'slain in the Spirit' at a touch from the evangelist's hand. Viewers were presented with statistics of thousands of converts and anecdotes of conversions and healings and asked for money to fund the programmes.

The electronic church was seen as the means of fulfilling the 'great commission' of taking the gospel via satellite to all the peoples of the world, which fundamentalists believe is necessary before the Second Coming of Christ. Naturally fundamentalist viewers opened their wallets and the wealth of the tele-evangelists increased. Big name tele-evangelists like Morris Cerullo, Kenneth Copeland, Pat Robertson, and Oral Roberts developed a theology which suggested or stated that it was God's intention for obedient Christians to be wealthy. Some went further and said that if viewers obeyed God by donating to their TV ministries, God would reward the donors financially. Cerullo has even suggested that getting him out of debt by pledging money will free God to solve the donors' own financial problems – he did not appear to consider giving his money away to free God to solve his financial problems.

Despite the fact that several tele-evangelists have been troubled by allegations of tax fraud, undignified legal wrangles or dalliances with prostitutes, they are still in the ascendant. Statistics have proven that tele-evangelism does not work in its stated aim of converting the masses, but tele-evangelists remain determined to save the world and continue in business. The sociologist Dr Steve Bruce has suggested that their main function (did they but know it) is to give somewhat paranoid fundamentalists some much needed self-esteem as they see their leaders daily on national television. However, it seems likely that since their audience is composed almost exclusively of fundamentalist Christians, tele-evangelists may have had considerable influence on the nature of fundamentalism in the USA. It is certainly true that the conservative fundamentalist constituency is an increasingly dogmatic, reactionary and paranoid ghetto, and as such they mirror many of their tele-evangelist heroes. While at the beginnings of the Charismatic revival in the UK the ghettoization of fundamentalists in the USA was well established, it is true to say that the more tawdry and tasteless exploits of tele-evangelists were still in their infancy. More importantly the nature and practice of Charismatic fundamentalists in the USA was not uncritically mimicked in the UK. Nevertheless, the influence of Charismatic fundamentalism in the USA on the Charismatic revival in the UK is significant and considerable, and it is important to appreciate the cultural background to this influence.

In Britain there are two distinct strands of what has been called the Charismatic movement. One remained doggedly outside the denominations; the other worked through all the main denominations, including non-evangelical and non-Protestant groups such as the Roman Catholic Church and the 'high church' (more liturgical, formal and ritualistic) Anglican congregations. Both strands came into being in the late 1950s and early 1960s, although the non-denominational strand only became prominent and distinct in the 1970s.

The Charismatic revival in the mainstream denominations was the first to attract media attention and was called the Renewal movement because participants saw themselves as renewing the Charismatic gifts to the denominations. It was linked to the earlier Pentecostal revival by an American Pentecostal, David du Plessis and Cecil Cousen, a British Pentecostal who had spent time in the USA with leaders of the Latter Rain movement – so-called because as Pentecostal fundamentalists they believed that in the end times God was giving a 'downpour' of the gifts of the Spirit on the church. Both du Plessis and Cousen were busy networking with like minded nascent Charismatics (of all and no denominations) around the country.

As Charismatics realized that they were not alone, they began arranging conferences and publishing pamphlets and magazines. By 1963 a movement was becoming established and the leaders were seeing it as God's visitation on the whole church rather than an reinvigoration of the increasingly stolid Pentecostal denominations. They were also encouraged to hear of Charismatic stirrings in mainline congregations in the USA, possibly in *Newsweek* or *Time* magazine which carried stories of high church Episcopalians speaking in tongues. Contacts with Americans outside the Pentecostal denominations were established. The Americans made an impression on the Anglican clergyman Michael Harper, who started convening meetings and sending circulars to sympathetic church people.

In 1964 Harper formed the Fountain Trust, and later, *Renewal* magazine in which he stated the Trust's aims. They were:

1. To encourage Christians of all churches to receive the power of the Holy Spirit and to glorify Christ by manifesting in their lives the fruits and gifts of the same Spirit, so that they may enrich their worship, strengthen their witness and deepen their fellowship.

2. To encourage local churches to experience renewal in the Holy Spirit and to recover full ministry of the Holy Spirit including that of healing.

3. To encourage Christians to expect and pray for worldwide revival.

A Charismatics' charter was thus established and it was clearly based on working through established denominations, beyond and including the Pentecostals. Indeed, when du Plessis visited London in 1964 he spoke of the gifts of the Spirit being practised by friends of his in the Roman Catholic Church. If for most American fundamentalists the Catholic Church was a front runner for anti-Christ status, this clearly was not du Plessis' view. The UK movement saw itself as ecumenical and as bringing the Holy Spirit to the whole church worldwide, without appearing to realize that their stress on the necessity of the gifts of the Spirit was likely, in itself, to cause division and possible sectarianism. Nevertheless, in this respect it was significantly different from fundamentalism in the USA.

It was, however, similar to fundamentalism in that it was 'experience'-based and thus, to some extent, subjective and anti-intellectual. Du Plessis himself said of receiving the Holy

Spirit: 'You come to the place where you do absolutely nothing but surrender totally to the Baptizer. That's how to get Baptism in the Holy Spirit . . . If your intellect has not gone under in the process, you're still holding out your intellect against the Holy Spirit.' There appears to have been little or no thought to the dangers of such an undertaking, particularly among unstable people. The belief in the Holy Spirit was such that it seemed inconceivable that this move of the 'spirit' could be damaging. However, the tone of the renewal movement was different from that of the fundamentalists in the USA, largely because it was working through old established denominations with a sense of their heritage and procedures, which acted as a check against excesses.

By the 1970s there were Charismatics throughout the denominations and they quickly became the fastest growing section of these denominations. *Renewal* magazine, which started with a circulation of hundreds, now boasts a circulation of 18,000. There are now Charismatic bishops and leaders across the denominations, principals of established theological colleges, politicians and police chiefs. The renewal part of the Charismatic movement has largely avoided the ghettoization of culture which happened with the US fundamentalists. Theologically they are also much looser and would generally object to the term fundamentalist.

The other sector of the Charismatic movement is known as the Restoration (or House Church) movement and has quite different aims. The term 'restoration' derives from the aim to restore God's kingdom on earth to what members see as unsullied New Testament perfection. They were as concerned as the Renewal movement to promote the practice of spiritual gifts, but thought that God's Kingdom was coming into Christendom outside the denominations and established churches. Initially, Restorationism was obscured by the Renewal movement, its members disaffected Brethren and Pentecostals.

By the late 1960s they were meeting in houses: worshipping, praying, speaking in tongues and practising the ministries of healing, deliverance and prophecy. Feeling estranged from the wider church, their small groups were characterized by close relationships and an intense expectation of God doing great things. The lack of any formal institutions and liturgy led to an anarchic rejection of what was seen as the restrictive legalism (the rules and structures) of the established denominations. Rules and set forms of worship were seen as placing a check on the Holy Spirit. Restorationists wanted the new wine of Charismatic gifts in new wineskins, and their churches were the wineskins.

The freedom and anarchy were short lived as the influence of a group of non-denominational Americans known as the Fort Lauderdale Five began to be felt. The Americans who visited and corresponded over a number of years were involved in a similar fundamentalist movement in Florida. They had also developed controversial theology known as 'shepherding' in which church leaders (known as 'apostles') developed a rigid hierarchy which placed people 'under' someone else's authority and spiritual direction to the extent that they had to confess sins to them and consult them over decisions. Shepherding was such that if your shepherd thought you were going out with the wrong person you had to come under their authority and break off the relationship or reject their 'covering' and leave the fellowship. The beginnings of this hierarchical and often heavy handed authority were in place before the Restorationists had contact with the Americans but the Fort Lauderdale Five gave them a clearer structure in which to operate it.

By the 1970s the house churches had outgrown their houses and were hiring school halls, warehouses and empty cinemas for their meetings. They also hosted large conventions, known as Bible weeks, which tens of thousands of Christians attended. Many Christians from mainline denominations were at these conventions and the Restorationists' confidence was such that they encouraged them publicly to leave the dead wood of denominationalism and join the new shoots of restoration. They saw themselves as part of a worldwide movement of the Spirit of God, building his Kingdom (through the church) outside the denominations.

It was at this point of burgeoning growth and confidence that the first signs of division among Restoration leaders occurred. Bryn Jones, one of the more forceful 'apostles', who led a network of churches largely in the north of England, felt that the leadership of some of the southern churches was too liberal, too equivocal about the 'world', too vague about what constituted sinful behaviour. There were a number of issues, but Gerald Coates, one of the more flamboyant, southern 'apostles', brought things to a head by stating that masturbation was not sin. In one meeting of a number of apostles Gerald Coates appears to have wanted them to admit that they all masturbated sometimes. The answer to this query never came out but it is clear that the northern apostles found it easier to admit to praying by themselves than playing by themselves.

Towards the end of 1976 the northern leaders sent a letter to their southern 'brothers' suggesting that they were falling into license and hinting that they might be being deceived by demons. A split occurred which remains to this day. The northern churches grew financially (with an efficient commercial wing, Harvest Time, selling Bible studies, tapes, gifts and other Christian paraphernalia) and in numbers. However, Bryn Jones left to further the movement's work in the USA, and the more authoritarian arm of the Restoration movement seems since to have foundered. They are no longer growing in numbers. Dr Andrew Walker of King's College, London, says: 'Restoration as a movement is finished. No second generation leaders emerged to take up the mantle. The problem was that shepherding produces sheep not leaders.'

However, the more liberal southerners, after a period in limbo, have continued to prosper and grow. Gerald Coates' Pioneer network of churches has recently bought an aircraft hangar to meet in. They have changed quite radically though. These days you will not find Coates calling people to leave the denominations. Now he shares a platform with Anglicans, Pentecostals and a broad spectrum of Charismatics; he no longer believes that the church is the non-denominational church worldwide. The authoritarian approach to shepherding has also been softened, the denominational exclusivity (that urged people to leave the 'dead wood of denominationalism') has been dropped and the more colourful language of apostleship seems to have faded. Basically, the Restoration movement has merged with the Renewal movement into a powerful, burgeoning movement promoting Charismatic gifts.

This was largely due to the rise of the Evangelical Alliance and an annual interdenominational worship and teaching conference, Spring Harvest. Although the Evangelical Alliance had existed for over 150 years, both the EA and Spring Harvest took off on the crest of the Charismatic wave. Spring Harvest was founded in

1979 by Clive Calver, then National Director of British Youth for Christ (until recently the General Director of the Evangelical Alliance), and Peter Meadows, a Charismatic Communications guru who edited *Buzz* magazine. Its aim was to bring together Charismatic Christians from all and no denominations to worship and learn together. They deliberately avoided sectarianism by ensuring that key teaching seminars were led by two or more speakers from different church backgrounds.

Spring Harvest's first year at Prestatyn attracted 2700 to a holiday camp during Easter week. The festival peaked in the mid-1980s with over 70,000 attending weekly conferences around the country held at Butlin's holiday camps. Spring Harvest largely succeeded in its aims. Leaders of large house churches, such as Coates and Roger Forster (who leads London's Ichthus fellowship), deepened friendships with denominational leaders and both groups realized that they were, in essence, doing the same thing, and would benefit from working together.

The massive growth of the Evangelical Alliance during the 1980s was both a symptom of the success of the Charismatic renewal as well as a unifying factor in the Charismatic movement. Although not all evangelicals (who define themselves as Bible believing) are Charismatic, the vast majority are. This was largely due to the effect of Spring Harvest and other evangelical/Charismatic rallies and conferences, which spread the message (and experience) of Charismatic gifts to a wider audience. The effect of Clive Calver (a non-practising Baptist minister), then the Evangelical Alliance's General Director, is hard to overestimate. As a leader, he was friendly, engaging, non-judgmental, and open minded. As a committed Charismatic who clearly values the evangelical tradition, he commands respect from a broad constituency of Charismatics and evangelicals. His tolerant and enthusiastic approach has done much to unify a movement which is historically given to sectarianism.

Calver has also helped to transform British Charismatics from a defensive constituency (which viewed social and political reform dimly and referred to it pejoratively as the 'social gospel') into a group with a mission which goes beyond winning souls and into social action as a worthwhile act in itself. He cites the evangelical reformers of the nineteenth century, such as Wilberforce, Shaftesbury, Booth and Barnardo, as his heroes. While remaining a convinced Charismatic (who attends Ichthus fellowship house church) he has placed social justice, unemployment and Third World and environmental issues at the heart of the Charismatic agenda. The appointment of George Carey as Archbishop of Canterbury in 1990 was another sign of the Charismatic movement's coming of age. Carey, the greatly respected churchman with a Charismatic heritage, also did much to extend the interests of Charismatics towards social and environmental issues.

It is probably no accident that this trend started during the individualistic Thatcherite 1980s. During that decade many Charismatics appeared to shed their judgmental and dualistic approach. Instead of seeing the 'world' as the enemy, the tendency was to see it as in need of reform because of injustices between rich and poor. Jesus' teachings on the poor (which far outnumber his pronouncements on Charismatic gifts) started to gain prominence. Tearfund, a relief and development agency started by the Evangelical Alliance, experienced a massive increase in donations in the 1980s and is now the sixth largest relief and development group in the UK.

Churches like Ichthus started employment projects and self-help groups for the unemployed and single mothers while lobbying the government for increased funding for the marginalized in society. Coates' Pioneeer churches were involved in caring for AIDS victims. CARE, a Christian support and lobbying organization, was active in working with single parent families and promoting Christian family values in government policy and education. Others organized relief convoys to refugee camps and orphanages in Romania and Kurdistan. The church was rediscovering its social conscience. As Calver says: 'We do not take on the agenda of American right-wing fundamentalists; we are often portrayed in this way but we are fighting for the weak in our society.'

However, despite the more progressive and liberal approach of Calver and others during the 1980s much of the Charismatic constituency remained conservative and somewhat paranoid and reactionary. One significant factor ensuring that Charismatics did not veer off from the supernatural way was the appearance in England of Mr Signs and Wonders himself, John Wimber. In many ways Wimber's appeal and influence was interesting and unusual. First, he was an American in a quite different mould from the tele-evangelists: gentle, genial, affable, more John Boy Walton than Newt Gingrich. He came with credentials from Fuller Church Growth seminary and had won a reputation as the leader of a burgeoning network of house church style groups, known as Vineyard. His Vineyard churches were active in evangelism as well as social projects. Wimber's teaching was not confrontational or dogmatic in style. All this made him more accessible to mainstream Charismatics (as opposed to more extreme and reactionary ones), yet his message was, arguably, extreme and one-sided.

At face value 1984 was not an auspicious time for Wimber to take the UK Charismatics by storm. A couple of years earlier the Revd David Watson, one of Britain's most prominent Anglican Charismatics, had died of cancer despite the fact that Watson had spent considerable time being prayed for by Wimber, or Mr Miracle as some called him. Wimber had believed that God would heal Watson until late on in Watson's life. Charismatics were confused: why had this man with a reputation for miracles not been instrumental in the healing of their respected and much-loved leader? At one of his preparatory meetings in London's Holy Trinity Brompton, Wimber was asked what had gone wrong. In view of the fact that he was a close friend of Watson, his answer was a testament to insensitivity and glibness: 'The devil won that battle but we're gonna make him pay.'

His meetings at Westminster Central Hall several months later were a massive success. His message was that the 'signs and wonders' mentioned in the Bible would show people that God was real and would lead to what Wimber called Power Evangelism. The concept was welcomed with open arms despite the fact that Jesus had rejected those seeking miraculous signs in His day. Wimber and his Vineyard teams toured the churches of Britain, expounding this teaching and then having a 'clinic' in which the Holy Spirit was asked to 'come down' and work. People collapsed, healings were claimed and the news of Power Healing and Power Evangelism swept the country. Perhaps buoyed up by their success, Wimber and his acolytes made some rather grand prophecies. Wimber prophesied that 50 per cent of cancer victims would be healed through his ministry: one can only imagine cancer sufferers at his meetings hoped that they were in the right 50 per cent. In the event they were not, but nobody noticed when they died.

Wimber's impact was such that the Wimber effect became known as the Third Wave, referring to the previous two 'waves' of Charismatic renewal (one at the beginning of the century and the second during the sixties). These days Wimber is the one in the wheelchair but the effect of Wimber and Vineyard churches is still massive, not least in the Toronto Blessing in which people collapse laughing or crying or making animal noises (usually roaring or mooing) on the floor, supposedly under the influence of the Holy Spirit. Several thousand churches now regularly experience the Toronto Blessing, although it has to be said that it has attracted criticism from some Charismatics. Nevertheless, the lasting effect of Wimber was to heighten the expectations of Charismatics that miracles would happen as a matter of course and, by implication, to sideline the social agenda put forward by Calver and other Charismatics. It has been argued that the supernatural 'signs and wonders' equip Charismatics to take on social action through refreshing them and giving them the internal resources to do so. Indeed, in Wimber's notes for a healing seminar, one of the manifestations of healing is 'sharing God's abundance with the oppressed poor'. However, the primary thrust of his teaching undoubtedly concentrates on healing from sickness, emotional healing and deliverance from demons. (He even talks of raising the dead!)

Not surprisingly, the Charismatic emphasis on miracles was reinvigorated. Despite the reformer's agenda that came from Calver and more progressive Charismatics, Charismatics in general were still highly preoccupied with the demonic and with deliverance. Scare stories of Satanic abuse (largely unfounded) were still being peddled by Charismatic Christians, leading to protracted court cases in Newcastle, Nottingham and the Orkneys, which were subsequently dropped. It is probably true to say that an unequivocal and dogmatic approach to abortion had always concerned Charismatics more than injustice and Third World issues. While ostensibly eschewing gay bashing, Charismatics maintained that same sex relationships involving intercourse were immoral and that homosexuals could often be healed. In addition to this there was still a thriving market for books, self-help guides, clothes and assorted paraphernalia which was indicative of a ghetto mentality and a fear and mistrust of the world.

This was the bedrock on which Calver and more liberal Charismatics had tried to establish a reformer's agenda and not surprisingly it was somewhat shaky. The desire to evangelize a fallen and squalid world and to show it the way was still strong, and to that extent a latent dogmatic and fundamentalist agenda was still in place. American evangelists like Morris Cerullo, Kenneth Copeland and Rodney Howard-Browne could still attract tens of thousands at venues like Earls Court, Westminster Central Hall and the National Exhibition Centre. It is equally unsurprising that factors which appear to have challenged, or at least subverted a more progressive Charismatic faith, came from the USA.

War in the Heavenlies

Hi-tech Battlefields

Rave music is pumping out of the speakers. The room is in semi-darkness, the lighting ambient, nightclub style. About a hundred young people are dancing, in dayglo and lycra dance wear, designer shirts, trainers and hair gel. They are ecstatic, letting it all go; sweating bodies and souls in unison. It could be a West End night club. In fact it is a church service.

Closer inspection reveals that many are dancing around their Bibles. The speakers in the centre of the room double as an altar. Indeed the £9000 sound system is primarily used as a means of encouraging Christians in their faith and evangelizing. Much of the music comes from the secular dance charts, but a careful listening reveals a litany of 'Christian' words such as spirit, soul and love – reinterpreted by the listeners as worship.

Terry Page, the leader of Chiswick-based Zoe Christian Fellowship, is a House Church leader unusually open to using contemporary culture as a means of getting the message across. Yet as he moves to the altar and picks up the microphone he chants 'You are not welcome here', pointing towards the left hand side of the building. The congregation do the same, chanting over the throbbing bass lines coming out of speakers from around the room. He turns to the right and repeats the ritual, eyes clenched closed and a commanding finger poking the air. The refrain is repeated over and over and then he points to the congregation and bellows, once again: 'You are not welcome here.'

A visitor to the church may well take it as a cue to leave the building, but the congregation is under no misapprehensions. They echo Pastor Page's commands with enthusiasm as hundreds stab the air with equal vehemence. They know that they are talking to demons not people and that they are cleansing the building of any evil spirits or Satanic powers that may be lurking.

They know that this is spiritual warfare and that with Jesus and the Holy Spirit they have the power to vanquish the enemy. The service continues, the congregation are untroubled by demonic interference as they pray in groups, dance and sing and take communion.

The scene is Spring Harvest at Butlin's in Minehead and over a thousand Charismatic Christians from all denominations are waiting to be addressed by Gerald Coates, the leader of a network of house churches known as Pioneer. They are elated after the hi-tech, guitar-based worship and are keen to hear what this gifted, eloquent and flamboyant leader has to say. He talks about the importance of the church accepting women in leadership, stating that thus far the absence of women in leadership has meant that the church is like an army of soldiers all with one arm behind their backs. He invites his wife, Anona, onto the platform and she delivers a part of the sermon.

When Anona has finished Coates talks about the shackles of Christian legalism (unnecessary and rigid rules) which make it unappealing to outsiders in our society. He talks specifically about many Christians' narrow and apparently judgmental attitude to drink, making it clear that he enjoys drinking without getting drunk. As he concludes his sermon he asks the thousand strong congregation to stand with him in prayer for the nation. They are instructed to raise their arms and pray against the spiritual powers in the heavenlies. Coates leads them in vanquishing the spiritual forces at the different points of the compass, explaining that dealing with demonic principalities in the atmosphere can have a tangible effect on terrestrial life as the spiritual forces lose their power over geographical areas. As they face the west, Coates leads them in prayers for the atmosphere over Westminster, and prays against any spiritual powers affecting the British government.

'Ye la to na socan, alea, noso', hums a thin, anoracked, bespectacled professional man. 'Uah laa calume, solome, aaarrgh', continues a large, smartly turned out black woman. A thirty-something blonde with a baby strapped to her takes up the cry: 'Me paca di soloso, kundara losso.' As the soothing chords fade, outstretched arms fall limp and the mellifluous sound of 11,500 people singing in tongues ebbs. A man with the snappy dress sense of a used car salesman walks to the front of the platform, takes the microphone and shouts, 'Hellooo Wembley.' Once again, it is Gerald Coates. He continues: 'Elton John, Prince, Madonna have all performed here but one day even they will have to bow their knees to Jesus Christ.'

The scene is the London For Jesus prayer rally at Wembley Arena. People have come to hear Korean revivalist, Yonggi Cho, the man with the largest church in the world (725,000), tell them how to do it in London. After the fifteen-piece band and Gerald Coates' rousing introduction there are other warm-up acts. Roger Forster, who leads the Ichthus network of churches in Lewisham, tells the story of Ichthus' battle with the Labour controlled borough council. Eight years ago, he explains, a memo went round the town hall instructing employees not to let properties to the church for services. This was because Ichthus had leafleted the borough opposing the council's policy of allowing gay couples to adopt children. Forster explained, 'Because we stood for family values, we met violent and vicious opposition.' The church then 'prayer-walked' every street in the borough, with particular concentration on the town hall.

Prayer-walking is simply walking and praying. The purpose of walking is to confront demonic spirits and powers en route who are vanquished by the presence of praying, 'spirit filled' Christians. According to the spiritual warfare teaching, which has its origins in the USA and South America, this changes things, not just in the heavenlies but here on earth, in town councils, banks, police stations, schools around the area. Eight years on, Forster concludes, the Mayor and other senior council leaders, the Chief Constable and Superintendent of Police are all Christians and Ichthus have a good relationship with the council from whom they rent several properties. The audience are on their feet: spontaneous applause.

Next, Colin Dye, who leads Kensington Temple, one of London's largest churches, invites the audience to enter into some 'spiritual warfare' for London. All those sitting in front of the stage are asked to pray against spirits of lawlessness and to banish them from the area, while those up in the 'gods' are asked to invite angelic spirits of law and order to inhabit the 'atmosphere' over London. Fighting with demonic and spiritual powers in prayer is clearly second nature to the congregation. They throw themselves into it shaking their fists at 'demons', stamping their feet, waving their arms angrily. Up above all is sweetness and light as those in the balcony speak in tongues, gently waving their arms attempting to waft in angelic powers. 'We declare the victory of Lord Jesus Christ against that lawless Spirit and banish you', concludes Colin Dye. A journalist friend with a twinkle in his eye whispers in my ear: ' Would it be possible to commit a crime in here?'

When the man with the world's largest church gets to the stage his message is simple: pray, it works. Cho describes a 'miracle' which occurred in his country when the communists were about to conquer South Korea. The ministers prayed for a miraculous weather change to allow US bombers to come to their aid; and lo, it was sunny and the heavens opened as hundreds of B29s flew in and carpet bombed the communists out of existence. 'But', Cho stresses, 'the battle was not won on the battleground, it was won in prayer.' He tells the congregation that victory is flowing from them, that revival is coming, that this is a turning point in UK history, that in government and society they 'will prevail against filth'. The whole event was a huge success, bringing some members of the platform to tears. But, of course, success was guaranteed, because unknown to the congregation, fifty 'prayer warriors' were hidden away in the basement battling it out with any recalcitrant demons lurking around Wembley Arena, trying to cramp God's style.

If that sounds like an obscure, extreme right-wing splinter group of Charismatic fundamentalists, it was not. On the platform were leaders of the UK's fastest growing churches, Clive Calver, Director of the Evangelical Alliance (which claims to represent two million Christians) and leaders of other national Christian charities and organizations; in the audience were Anglicans, Methodists and a few Roman Catholics alongside the more typical Pentecostalists and House Churches members.

Not surprisingly, many theologians and church leaders have voiced considerable doubts about the doctrine of spiritual warfare, particularly in relation to its potential for leading to a paranoid, illusory world view in which demons are perceived to be everywhere. However, what is noticeable about the three examples of spiritual warfare mentioned above is that in each instance those engaged in spiritual warfare appear to be, at least in some ways, unusually relaxed about aspects of our culture which the pentecostal Charismatics a generation earlier would have considered demonic or, at best, 'worldly'. Pastor Page's use of dance music, Coates' drinking and endorsement of the leadership of women, and Forster's interest and involvement in local politics, would all have been frowned upon thirty years ago.

It is possible that this reflects an increased confidence on the part of Charismatics as they appropriate the methods and technology of modern culture and use it to get their message across. It does not appear to reflect a breaking down of the barrier between saved and unsaved as the language of spiritual warfare shows. Apart from phrases like 'opposing filth' at the London For Jesus rally, the language of spiritual warfare involves Christian prayer warriors engaging in battle with principalities, demons, and spiritual powers located in the skies (or atmosphere) over geographical areas. The language in songs and prayers and books about spiritual warfare is largely about opposition. It is bombastic, triumphalist and militaristic. Prayer warriors do not walk, they march; they seem to prefer proclaiming to praying; claiming (or 'taking hold of') is preferred to asking or petitioning. This kind of language harks back to the dogmatic and dualistic American fundamentalists of the 1950s. The world is no longer a neutral place to be judged on its merits in differing situations, it is a place to be viewed with suspicion. If it is not the enemy, it is at least tainted by him, under his influence and seeking to harm Christians. So while utilizing the hi-tech paraphernalia of the 'world', many modern Charismatics still view it with in-built distrust, sometimes verging on paranoia.

Origins of Conflict

So if these are the concepts and practices of spiritual warfare, where did they originate? Once again, the actual source of these beliefs was an interpretation of some passages from the Bible. They were based largely on the passage in the letter to the Ephesians, a letter whose central message was a plea for Christian unity:

> Finally be strong in the Lord and in his mighty power.
> Put on the full armour of God so that you can take
> your stand against the devil's schemes. For our

struggle is not against flesh and blood, but against the rulers, against the authorities, against the powers of this dark world and against the spiritual forces of evil in the heavenly realms. Therefore put on the whole armour of God, so that when the day of evil comes, you may be able to stand your ground, and after you have done everything, to stand. Stand firm then, with the belt of truth buckled round your waist, with the breastplate of righteousness in place, and with your feet fitted with the readiness that comes from the gospel of peace. In addition to all this, take up the shield of faith, with which you can extinguish all the flaming arrows of the evil one. Take the helmet of salvation and the sword of the Spirit, which is the word of God. And pray in the Spirit on all occasions with all kinds of prayers and requests.

(Ephesians 6:10-18)

Throughout history Christians have struggled against the powers of evil, also called the devil. But traditionally this has been understood as resisting temptation and challenging unjust practices personally, socially and politically. This struggle has been described in colourful language by many Christians, and has been understood literally by some and metaphorically by others. Yet there has been more to the Christian understanding of the universe than just God and the devil. In *Pilgrim's Progress*, Bunyan's pilgrim is constantly tempted to leave The Way. He sinks in the Slough of Despond (depression), dallies at Vanity Fair (vanity), and passes Doubting Castle (doubt or uncertainty). Before reaching the Celestial City, Christian is also frightened by chained roaring lions (based on the description of the devil as a 'roaring lion' in Peter's first epistle). Bunyan's allegory includes demonic figures as well as personifications of natural human situations (like doubt or depression) which Christian faced.

A wide range of Christian writers (Ignatius Loyola, Thomas à Kempis, Luther and C. S. Lewis) testify to struggling with the devil (usually in the form of temptation), but see the world as the arena for the struggle, neither wholly good (or Godly) nor wholly bad (or diabolical). It has been seen as a mixture and in many areas (such as language, culture, communications) is considered neutral. Indeed the author of James' epistle clearly has a concept of the middle area when he says: 'When tempted no-one should say "God is tempting me." For God cannot be tempted by evil, nor does he tempt anyone; but each one is tempted when, by his own evil desire, he is dragged away and enticed.'

The advent of the type of spiritual warfare described earlier is a significant move away from the traditional Christian position. It is largely true of the recent interpretations of spiritual warfare teaching that they ignore the middle area and divide everything between diabolical and divine. Theologically this is known as 'dualism' (between God and the devil); nothing is seen as neutral, it either has the stench of Satan or the fragrance of God. Although fringe evangelicals and Charismatics have always had a very pronounced dualism, it is only within the last decade that such beliefs have become widespread. Perhaps it should be no surprise that the writings of three Americans have been the major agents of change in this area.

The influence of John Wimber's ministry in the mid-1980s was significant. In the notes to his *Healing Seminar*, Wimber writes of the understanding of healing in the New Testament: 'Sickness is seen to be an extension of sin, and therefore it is evil in origin and is a representation of the Kingdom of darkness.' In classically dualistic terms, he continues: 'We shall see that in the coming of Jesus, the Kingdom of God came with great power to confront and overcome sickness, sin, death and the devil.' Indeed Wimber has said that Jesus 'saw an integral unity between sickness and Satan'. As the theologian Nigel Wright says: 'John Wimber comes close to an unwholesome dualism by suggesting that the earth is Satan's territory rather than the Lord's, by reading biblical texts as though they are references to Satan when this is not necessary, and by eclipsing from our view the realm of the natural . . . In relation to sickness, a clearer focus is gained when it is viewed as the consequence of disorder in the natural realm.' Wright saw the dualism of Wimber's 'Signs and Wonders' movement as giving too high a profile to the ideas of 'Satan' and to spiritual warfare.

Meanwhile, in 1986 a book was published in the USA (and later in the UK) which was to popularize the doctrine of spiritual warfare more effectively than the most thoroughgoing theological treatise or healing campaign. Frank Peretti's novel *This Present Darkness* was an absolute blockbuster, selling hundreds of thousands in America alone – in Britain 25, 000 copies of *This Present Darkness* and its sequel, *Piercing the Darkness,* have been sold. In it a world is described where everything happening in the lives of the inhabitants of the sleepy little town of Ashton reflects a titanic struggle between demonic principalities and godly angels in the heavenlies above the town. In a racy, cliché ridden style, the books suggested a dualism, a spiritual battle with no neutral ground. A passage early on in the book, where a demon tries to enter a church service (to be met by an angel), illustrates this:

> With an eerie cry of rage and indignation, it gathered itself up off the sidewalk and stared at the strange door that would not let it pass through. Then the membranes on its back began to billow, enfolding great bodies of air, and it flew with a roar headlong at the door, into the foyer – and into a cloud of white hot light. The creature screamed and covered its eyes, then felt itself being grabbed by a huge, powerful vice of a hand. In an instant it was hurling through space like a rag doll, outside again, forcefully ousted.

The effect of *This Presesent Darkness* was phenomenal. It introduced hundreds of thousands of Christian novel readers to an extreme theological position which only diehard students of prayer and spiritual warfare would be familiar with. There is evidence that many of the readers began to take the contents seriously in relation to their Christian lives. It was a watershed, a moment of critical mass, for the doctrine of spiritual warfare. As one of spiritual warfare's main protagonists, Dr Peter Wagner, says: 'Undoubtedly, the single most influential event that has stimulated interest in strategic-level spiritual warfare among American Christians was the publication of Frank Peretti's two novels, *This Present Darkness* and *Piercing the Darkness.* Many Christians who had scarcely given a thought to the possibility that events shaping human society could have a relationship to struggles among powerful supernatural beings are now openly talking about the likelihood.'

Dr Wagner (and his colleagues at Fuller Theological Seminary, California – where Wimber also taught for some time) became the third major catalyst by creating a dualistic theology with spiritual warfare at its heart. Wagner, a church growth expert, began studying the 'spiritual dimensions' of church growth, particularly what he called 'strategic level spiritual warfare'. He was particularly interested in church growth in Argentina, a country which had at that time resisted the spread of Charismatic Protestantism which had affected the bulk of Latin American countries.

An Argentinian pastor, Eduardo Lorenzo, working in Adrogue, a wealthy suburb of Buenos Aires, interested Wagner. Lorenzo's church had not been growing until he started practising spiritual warfare. They 'discerned' a spiritual power over the Adrogue area and began fasting, praying, and interceding against the spirit. As Wagner says: 'Almost the entire congregation joined together for strategic-level intercession. They took authority over the principality over the city and the lesser demonic forces. At 11:45 that evening they collectively felt something break in the spiritual realm. They knew the battle was over. The evil spirit had left, and the church began to grow.'

Carlos Annacondia was another Argentinian who greatly interested Wagner. The long term results of Annacondia's evangelistic crusades are statistically much better than those of his contemporaries like Billy Graham or Morris Cerullo. The churches also seem to experience revival following his visits. The reason according to Wagner is that Annacondia engages in battle with the spirits over the cities that he visits before he preaches. Only when they sense that the battle has been won in the heavenlies will evangelism (and deliverance or exorcism) begin. Wagner believes Annacondia may turn out to be the most effective crusade evangelist of all time. Indeed, in true spiritual warfare parlance, he says: 'It was probably no coincidence that the day he launched his first public crusade was the day the British sank the Argentinian battleship *General Belgrano* in the 1982 Falkland Islands War.' The idea being, one assumes, that the effect of his ministry on the spiritual powers in the heavenlies allowed the British torpedo to find its mark. One wonders whether the mothers of the soldiers on board share the same belief. But as Wagner bullishly says: 'There are casualties in spiritual warfare.'

Gradually, Wagner and like minded Charismatics developed a detailed theology of spiritual warfare, stressing the existence of a hierarchy of demons and Satanic powers which inhabited anything from an ornament on the mantelpiece, to a building, geographical area or nation. In what he calls a 'case study' (others would call it an anecdote) of spiritual territoriality, Wagner relates the stories of a missionary working with a tribe of Mexican Indians who also believed demons had specific areas and powers. The point being that these un-Christianized Indians believed in spirits with authority over certain physical areas, and that this backed up his theories. Wagner also believes that it is important that demons are named. He cites the fairy tale of Rumpelstiltskin (who he says is clearly a demonic power) and explains how once the king's bride discovered Rumpelstiltskin's name, his curse was broken.

'Spiritual mapping' is another concept embraced by Wagner and others at Fuller Theological Seminary. In essence this means mapping an area to show what the diabolical and divine influences on it are. A recipe for rampant fundamentalist nationalism? Well perhaps it is not surprising that the two Americans working in the area located the Middle East and north Africa as under Satanic influence. Luis Bush, of the evangelistic organization AD2000, locates the centre of the diabolical between the latitudes of 10 and 40 degrees. He has drawn a rectangle round it, which he calls the '10/40 window'. As George Otis, Jr, a computer-based spiritual mapper for the Sentinel Group, says: 'The lands and societies of the 10/40 window can hardly avoid becoming the primary spiritual battleground of the 1990s and beyond. And when the epic conflict finally unfolds, enemy operations will in all likelihood be managed from two powerful strongholds – Iran and Iraq – situated at the epicentre of the window.'

It is probably worth reminding oneself that the purpose of spiritual warfare is effective evangelism. In the same pragmatic way that Wimber saw 'signs and wonders' as a tool for evangelism, so exponents of spiritual warfare are clear that the end is effective worldwide evangelization. Iran and Iraq are targeted not because of their politics but because of their religion and their geographical position, at the heart of what the 'spiritual mappers' see as un-Christian geographical areas. Nevertheless, one has to ask questions when American Christians supposedly dispassionately locate Baghdad and Tehran as the epicentres of evil. After all, two decades earlier, Hal Lyndsey, in his best-selling book *The Late Great Planet Earth* located the anti-christ and t he final conflict in the Soviet Union. Is it even worth asking whether this is home-spun nationalistic racism or state of the art theology?

This pragmatic approach to evangelism (the idea that it works after spiritual warfare victories have been won) is also reflected in Wagner's book *Warfare Prayer*. In a chapter entitled *The Rules for City Taking*, the third rule is: 'Project a clear image that the effort is not an activity simply of Pentecostals and Charismatics, but of the whole body of Christ.' What Wagner means by this, amounts to using what appears to be 'sleight of hand' to encourage non-Charismatics to engage in spiritual warfare. If spiritual warfare is projected as broad-based and orthodox, the hope is that more traditional Christians will join in without asking too many questions about what they are doing. It has to be said that Wagner and his colleagues have succeeded in these aims in ways that are quite staggering.

Marching as to War

Following the teaching of Wimber, Peretti and Wagner, a London-based organization took up the spiritual warfare torch and spread it around the world with phenomenal success. The March For Jesus organization has proved more successful than even its most flamboyant and optimistic leaders could have imagined. The ideas behind the march started with Roger Forster's inner city Ichthus Christian Fellowship. As Forster explains of Icthus marches during the mid-1980s, in *March For Jesus: the official story*: 'It was in those early days that I began to notice that a change took place when we were more public and visible. I was aware that something was happening in the heavens as we were doing things on earth. The awareness was subjective, but others also sensed that we were affecting the spiritual condition of the area simply by being out in the open and witnessing before heaven and earth.' Perhaps following the leads of Annacondia and the Argentinian Christians, by engaging in spiritual warfare before evangelizing, Forster and his congregation 'prayer-walked' before trying to establish new congregations or 'church plants' in particular areas. On one occasion they were told that the activities of a local witches' coven were restricted because of the effect of an open air event. In 1986 Ichthus decided to take on Soho, the centre of the sex industry in London. They sang and prayed round the area, stopping to pray for specific places. As Forster relates: 'Not more than a few weeks later, the Westminster police raided Soho and shut down all the illicit, unlicensed sex shops and shows. We believe it was part of the process of bringing the presence of God, by the Holy Spirit in his people, into the area.'

The following year, Forster got together with Gerald Coates (of the Pioneer network of churches), Lynn Green (Director of an evangelistic organization, Youth With a Mission) and the Ichthus member and Charismatic songsmith, Graham Kendrick. They met to plan a march based on a vision which they shared. All four were Charismatics with a similar view of spiritual warfare. The first March For Jesus was limited to 15,000 marchers, largely members of Charismatic churches in London and the South East. They marched through the City, Britain's financial centre, on May 23rd, praying against the influence of greed and corruption in the banking and financial institutions. As it said in their prayer script to be read by leaders along the way: 'The stock exchange and many banks represent what Jesus says can be an alternative to God – mammon. We don't wish to see them leading the wild race of consumerism and greed down the Gadarene slope of self destruction. We need to challenge the spiritual forces that lie behind their wrong use of wealth.'

The script was quite open about their purpose: 'To some it will be an introduction to spiritual warfare, to others the opportunity to do something positive in the solidarity of God's people to change the supernatural atmosphere of our country.' They believe that five months later they got results. Black Monday, on October 19th, saw global panic as share prices plummeted in the City and on Wall Street. The March For Jesus leaders saw this as God acting in response to their vanquishing of the demonic forces in the City. As they say in *March For Jesus: the official story*: 'At a stroke £50 billion was wiped off City stock values and by the end of the week they had dropped nearly £102 billion. We praised God that changes were taking place.' The 'superstitions' or 'prayer principles' of Frank Peretti's novels were becoming actuality.

Following subsequent marches, equally grandiose claims were

made. Coates, who says he believes in seeing history with 'prophetic eyes' has also explained the 1988 hurricane and Mrs Thatcher's dismissal from office as human fallout from the spiritual battles effected during the marches. He explains the battle in the heavenlies thus: 'There's another dynamic which is the supernatural. When one lifts one's hands over certain areas, one's raised hands are a prophetic act. If Jesus can cast out demons, through prayer, move dark forces, forces from persons, areas, structures and institutions, it's not sensationalizing spiritual warfare to call it corporate exorcism.'

This corporate exorcism is not understood as metaphorical; it is seen as vanquishing actual demons whose nature or personality reflects the spirit or atmosphere of the place. However, as the marches experienced exponential growth rates (from 15,000 to 200,000 in two years) the language of spiritual warfare was toned down. Perhaps aware of Wagner's advice to try and include a broad cross-section of Christians in *Rules For Taking A City*, praise and the importance of Christian unity were stressed at the expense of the language of spiritual warfare. Explaining to an increasingly broad spectrum of Christians (Charismatic and non-Charismatic) that they were involved in corporate exorcism was going to be difficult. Coates explains: 'We were looser with our language in the past, without realizing that there's a whole crowd of Christians who could not cope with it. We had to learn that although we believe in casting out of demons and proclaiming the gospel to shift dark forces or Satan, these people do not use our phraseology.'

If the more muted language was intended to encourage non-Charismatics and to boost the numbers of marchers, it worked. First it spread to Europe, then the USA, and in 1994 March For Jesus went around the globe. The 1994 march was interesting for a number of reasons. It was predicted that there would be a march in every capital city of every country. If the country's regime was hostile to public Marches For Jesus (as they surely would be in that '10/40 window' and elsewhere) then a clandestine event would be held indoors. According to a Global March promotional video it was to be a day to change the world.

Dr Peter Wagner said on this video that it was to be one of the most powerful events in Christian history. Although the spiritual warfare theology underpinning the march was played down,

Wagner believed that prayer on such a scale was going to herald revival. He said, in something approaching a 'prophecy': 'I am believing God that 30 per cent of the world's committed Christians will be praying in a synchronized, coordinated way for the evangelization of the world. That means 160 million individuals will be praying that day.' The idea was that as the warfare prayer went round the timezones the demonic powers would be ushered off the planet or, at least, severely restricted in what they could do to oppose evangelism. Wagner predicted: 'The world after June 25th 1994 will never be the same and the gospel will spread as it never has before.'

In the event there were only 12 million marchers, but they were spread around approximately 170 nations. No doubt Wagner and other students of spiritual warfare and church growth are busy finding statistics to fit their predictions but it seems likely that the rest of the world is oblivious to the fact that it has changed. The Charismatic church is growing rapidly worldwide but it also appears to have 'peaked' in many countries and exactly how church growth relates to June 25th 1994 is unclear. The kind of revival that Wagner and others were predicting would, one assumes, be on the sort of scale that people would notice. Nevertheless the around-the-world March For Jesus can now be legitimately be called the world's largest Christian 'event'.

Another interesting development linked with March For Jesus and spiritual warfare is Challenge 2000. This organization, run by the son of the March For Jesus leader, Roger Forster, is the first UK-based attempt at using demographic computer-based technology in spiritual warfare. Following on from the 'spiritual mapping' work of American organizations like AD2000 and the Sentinel Group, it aims to produce a database which holds marketing profiles of geographical areas as well as spiritual mapping charts. This unusual mixture of hi-tech and fundamentalist dualism is, Chris Forster believes, at the cutting edge of church growth in the UK. The Challenge 2000 database is recording demographic information based on the government census and using it as a marketing company would, to locate what type of people live in particular environments and what their needs and aspirations are. This information is fed through to churches in particular areas to see how they can best serve their constituency and what methods of evangelism seem most appropriate. Indeed the Christian-designed computer programme is so successful as a demographic and marketing tool that secular companies are now using it.

In addition, evangelistic organizations and churches can feed their data back so that, according to Challenge 2000's Director, Chris Forster, they can record which streets have been 'given the gospel' and which are still virgin territory. March For Jesus is the main organization to use the database so far but, other evangelistic organizations and church groups are beginning to get involved. March For Jesus' 1995 campaign was called Operation A to Z as if they had the Challenge 2000 geographical project in mind. Their aims dovetail with the database. March For Jesus '95 aimed to see each house in the country prayed for. After the march, data were sent back to Challenge 2000 so that they could show geographically the extent to which areas are prayed for and thus cleansed of demonic influence. By recording prayer for an area or 'prayer tracking' on computer, the colours on the monitor showed the extent to which the enemy has been vanquished, assuming that they do not come across an enemy stronghold which needs additional prayer. Once the demonic influence is dealt with, the theory goes, people are then ready to respond to evangelism.

Although there have been voices in the wilderness arguing that such hi-tech spiritual warfare is fantasy, they have not had much impact on these organizations. It seems that this new triumphalism is in the ascendant in the Charismatic church worldwide. Yet the critics have pertinent and disturbing observations. Dr Andrew Walker, Lecturer in Education and Theology at King's College, London, has called the current practice of spiritual warfare delusory, paranoid and potentially dangerous. He says: 'Much of the recent reinterpretation of spiritual warfare has no basis in the Bible. The idea that by praying, marching or proclaiming, they can somehow shift the demonic atmosphere over geographical areas is silly. The idea that this will solve the problems of unemployment, moral decay or ecological disaster, beggars belief.' Canon Michael Saward has also criticized the theology of spiritual warfare as manifested in March For Jesus as an extreme and tendentious interpretation of the Bible. He recommended that his parish boycott the march because he believed it was an ill-judged act of corporate exorcism.

Dave Tomlinson, who leads Holy Joes, a 'church' for disaffected evangelicals and Charismatics, which meets in a pub in Brixton, suggests that the extreme dualism is the most worrying aspect of spiritual warfare. He says: 'The tendency in this new teaching is to see the church as all good and the world as all bad; they fail to see that there's a lot of good in the world and a lot of the devil in the church.' Tomlinson suggests that low self-esteem may be the motivating factor behind strident and extreme theologies of spiritual warfare. 'Evangelicals and Charismatics have long suffered from an inferiority complex and however much they try to hype it up, the Charismatic movement has not delivered, the dead have not been raised, revival has not swept the nation. It may well be this sense of fear and frustration that has led them to take the Christian agenda away from the real world and into the heavenlies.'

Although this may render them ridiculous and irrelevant, Tomlinson is concerned that this simplistic world view could be attractive for the insecure and the bigoted. 'On the one hand,' he says, 'it allows people with problems to escape from them; on the other hand this judgmental and triumphalist theology is more dangerous in the hands of narrow minded leaders.' He believes that homophobia, religious intolerance and other forms of prejudice could result, and claims to have come across scores of people who have been damaged by what appears to be a judgmental 'black and white' approach. He says: 'I've known several people facing religious crises either because they could not cope with the dogmatism of their faith or because they were paranoid and guilty, seeing the devil round every corner.' He is scathing concerning the effects of spiritual warfare on contemporary Christianity: 'As a positive approach to life in modern society, it's a non-starter. As evangelism, it's hard to think of anything less attractive than fundamentalist black and white dogmatism with a ludicrous bit of demonbusters theology thrown in.'

Prophets and Losses

Jeremiah was a prophet spitting in the wind. He was railing against his culture and pointing to what he thought God was telling him was a better way. He did not mind hurling invective, unfurling a prophetic abyss and getting it all back in his face. If this was benediction, to those around him it sounded like malediction. Like most Old Testament prophets he was concerned with injustice and idolatry, with a nation losing its way. Although there are prophecies in the Old and New Testaments that appear to offer 'psychic' insights into the future or into people's lives, the predominant Christian view of prophecy has traditionally had more to do with challenging society than with exercising Christian clairvoyance. Wilberforce, Bonhoeffer, Martin Luther King and Archbishop Desmond Tutu would appear to fit the prophetic mould of the ancients.

The Charismatic church's practice of 'prophecy' appears to have reversed this. Prophecy against injustice is more likely to be viewed with suspicion, whereas the practice of a sort of Christian clairvoyance (in which 'God' predicts the future), under the auspices of the Holy Spirit, has become predominant. One might expect that these prophecies would present the 'prophets' with too obvious a 'hostage to fortune' (in that the speaker's reputation might be seen to rest on the prophecy's fulfillment) and that this would stop, or at least discourage, the utterances. They do not. Perhaps under the influence of hyper-ventilation following too many choruses, the 'prophets' from the platform prophesy with conviction, authority and sincerity. In one to one situations, they are often more specific in their 'insights' and equally convinced that God has a direct line into their psyche. Public and private prophecies have very different dynamics, although obviously the former generally attract more publicity. Both merit examination, though private prophecies will be dealt with in the next chapter.

There have been countless prophecies from public platforms concerning physical ailments, the activities of the devil or the proximity of revival. To onlookers the subject matter of such prophesies may appear to say more about the concerns of the 'prophet' than about the current interests of the divine. One church leaders' meeting in Sheffield, shortly after the Bosnian ceasefire, appeared completely unruffled after hearing 'God' tell them that the devil had moved his headquarters from central Bosnia to inner city Sheffield. Perhaps they interpreted the fall of the radical Nine O'clock Service as confirmation of the prophecy. At any rate, would-be prophets can take comfort from the short memory of Charismatics. It is very rare for prophets to be publicly confronted with their errors. This may be because a sort of blurring of boundaries occurs in which people speak prophetically without actually calling it a prophecy. Hence Yonggi Cho, the Korean pastor of the world's largest church, can announce (in prophetic manner) a major spiritual turning point for the UK (see Chapter 3) and nobody will hold him account-able for his words when nothing happens. There appears to be a reluctance to confront 'prophets' about their predictions.

One major exception to this occurred with a group known as the Kansas City Prophets, a self-proclaimed group of 'prophets' based in Kansas, who predicted a number of things and who were publicly challenged about them by a local minister. Paul Cain, one of these prophets closely associated with John Wimber, made a prophecy about a revival that would 'break out' in London in October 1990. John Wimber took his family over to witness the event. October came and went and the weather got colder. When nothing happened, a revisionist version of the 'prophecy' was offered. People were told that Cain had merely spoken of 'tokens' of revival as a harbinger of the real thing. Perhaps because John Wimber and the Kansas City Prophets had such a prominent platform in Charismatic circles, some UK theologians and church leaders raised questions about these alleged prophecies, asking for a public apology or statement of error. As surely as the prophet's predictions never occurred, neither did an apology. The effect of creating such false expecta-tions among Charismatic Christians might be expected to generate disillusionment. However (and perhaps this is more telling), the predominant tendency is to forget and to continue until the next big name, offering Charismatic experience or portents of revival, comes to town. It is because of this that the activities of 'prophets' and the consequences of 'prophecy' need considering in relation to their potential to exploit or control people.

Morris Cerullo writes in the prophetic mode to thousands of his supporters in the UK, offering them 'God's promised benefits and victories' in return for money. He appears to be selling step by step miracles, 'spiritual breakthroughs', the conversion of vast numbers of Jews (according to Cerullo a pre-requisite for Christ's return), on the basis of his 'prophecies'. While living in his luxurious house in the exclusive La Jolla district of San Diego, his tasteless and lurid mailshots seek financial support from his support base of working class Pentecostals. One of his letters started:

> Dear Beloved in Christ,
>
> God has shown me by the gift of discernment of spirits that Satan has launched an attack against 7 separate areas of your life . . . 7 weeks – 7 steps – 7 miracles . . . never has God made such a major declaration, such a clear promise for his endtime people!

The letters contained phrases linking the fulfillment of the 'prophecy' with a financial gift. In his second letter Cerullo stated: '*Give your sacrificial gift* and activate God's promise for your life. Release the largest sacrificial gift you can possibly give. As you give $12 or even 25, God will honor His promise. Make it a gift that costs you something.'

By his seventh letter, his seven miracles (household salvation, household deliverance, God's physical healing, financial deliverance and new vision of Endtime rewards and others) had unfolded and Cerullo was focusing on sacrificial giving. His prophecies were as grand as ever ('I prophesy that in the next six years – before the year 2000 – more souls will be won to Christ than in the total history of Christianity') and, predictably, linked with financial giving. Cerullo urged his followers to broaden their vision, to forget about paying the rent as they asked for a house of their own. 'It's time', Cerullo wrote, 'to see the God of Abraham – supplying more than enough . . . flowing a miracle of finances into your life.'

In November 1995 Cerullo claimed that God had told him to

fast for ten days for the families of his followers. He circulated a three step 'Family Title Deed' in which he encouraged his followers to fill in all the needs for their families. Step One was to fill in all their family concerns on a printed card (unsaved members, drug and financial problems, frictions, broken relationships), Step Two was to write a cheque to Morris Cerullo World Evangelism and Step Three was to send both off in the prepaid envelope. Cerullo promised: 'During my ten days of fasting and prayer, I will take this family deed in my hands and I will personally pray for every need in your family, coming against Satan's attacks on them.'

In the next few weeks four similar mailings were sent out, and Cerullo's 'hunger strike' was extended to twenty one days, as his fundraising letters cum 'prophecies' continued. Some time later he appeared to stretch bounds of good taste even further, with his 'Confidential Messiah Project'. On the envelope he named a Jew needing the donor's sponsorship to receive the Christian message. It read: 'Sima Gartenberg needs Mr Howard's sponsorship to receive The Messiah!' Many Charismatics found such mailshots tasteless and immoral and, after a number of complaints, the Evangelical Alliance decided to take action. Cerullo's membership of the Evangelical Alliance had been constantly 'under review' because of his prosperity teaching (a doctrine which claims that part of a Christian's inheritance is wealth by right) and his fundraising letters. In October 1996 a confidential vote was taken and the Evangelical Alliance unanimously decided that he should be expelled. Within days he voluntarily stood down from the Evangelical Alliance but, he stressed, there was no connection. He simply wanted to stand down. However, there were consequences for the Evangelical Alliance: the Pentecostal church, Kensington Temple, the largest church in Britain, left the organization in protest.

Perhaps it is no surprise that when Cerullo, the prophetic fundraiser, predicts what his money will be used for, he seems to lack divine insight. Cerullo raised £600,000 to launch a European Christian satellite TV channel (on the Astra satellite) with a launch date of August 1992. A year later his representatives were claiming that transmission was months away. Greg Mauro, Morris Cerullo World Evangelism's European Director, said: 'I have a contract that's in place, that's signed, that is valid.'

However, TV companies beaming off the Astra satellite denied having contact with Cerullo, although the Children's Channel claimed that they had been in contact a year earlier but that the plans to broadcast had been dropped. When confronted with this, Mauro admitted that the agreement was unlikely to be consummated, and said that the £600,000 was in the bank. Would the people who faithfully donated to Cerullo's satellite station be reimbursed? 'That is a no win question', Mauro said. Five years later there is no sign of Cerullo beaming his prophecies down on us and, presumably, his donors are to believe that their monies are still in the bank.[1]

In the USA, Cerullo's donors and business partners have had some questions about exactly what he uses his money for. In 1980 an eighty year old widow, Merle L. gave $70,000 and her farm, which was sold for several hundred thousand dollars. She thought that her money was being used for a Christian cause but was surprised to discover that at least £100,000 of the money was put in a trust fund and loaned to desperate businessmen at lucrative interest rates. Cerullo has also used MCWE (Morris Cerullo World Evangelism) funds in real estate transactions and for loans to family members. In 1991, Yet King Loy, then Cerullo's Malaysian business partner in the Heritage Christian theme park, sued him for taking money raised for the Heritage project. Loy said, 'He used the Heritage name to appeal for money for the Heritage facilities. The money was taken and he kept the money.'

There have been other abortive projects based on Cerullo's prophetic ministry. The 'vision' for his much vaunted World Outreach Centre in San Diego lasted three years and collapsed in 1981 when he was sued by builders, estate agents and senior citizens who had given their homes to MCWE. Despite the distinctly worldly nature of many of Cerullo's activities his UK supporters refuse to ask questions. He is free to prophesy and to profit.[2]

There are 'prophets' with a more sophisticated approach. Cerullo's 'prophetic' utterances on the personal lives of the conservative Charismatic heartland are simple and direct. Others succeeded in fusing apparently 'psychic' prophetic insight with the more idealistic reformer's mode of prophecy. Steve Williams was a youth leader in St Thomas' Sheffield when John Wimber came to town. He was involved with a radical left of centre experiment at creating Christian community in inner city Sheffield. It was following a 'prophecy' from Robert Warren (he felt that God was telling him that he wanted to fill his church with 200 young people), team rector of St Thomas', that it was decided to set up the now infamous 'rave church', the Nine O'clock Service, under the leadership of Chris Brain. Williams was Brain's assistant, with pastoral responsibility for the congregation.

After Wimber's visit, Brain had close contact with Wimber and his associates, the Kansas City Prophets. The fledgling congregation embraced Wimber's notion of prophecy, and some of the prophecies of the Kansas City prophets left leaders fearing for their lives or eternal destiny. 'It was frightening at times, we believed that these men had a direct line from God and when they prophesied or spoke about the consequences of our evil, we took it seriously', Williams says. The Revd Chris Brain had always had a prophetic ministry in the sense that people thought that his radical urban and artistic vision was prophetic (it was seen as challenging and had much to say to the staid middle class church), but, after Wimber's visit, he started to use Charismatic prophecy to tell people what was going to happen to them or what God wanted to say to them.

Williams says that Brain felt constantly threatened by the leaders working under him. 'He regularly asked me about other leaders and whether they were trying to usurp his leadership; he challenged all of us about power seeking', Williams says. Then Brain started 'prophesying' to the leaders about their alleged attempts at undermining him. His prophecies sometimes came through 'pictures' and one of his pictures was of himself on a throne with his leaders trying to clamber over him. Williams remembers him interpreting this in two ways. 'He approached us and told us that we were ambitious, we were desperate to dominate and lead the Nine O'clock Service, and he was being told to assert his leadership, to speak and lead with greater authority', Williams recalls. He told the leaders that they were to acknowledge him as their sole leader and founder; this was the mantle that God was urging him to take, he said.

The effect on the leadership team was dramatic. At the next congregational meeting (a monthly meeting to discuss church issues) Williams counted the number of times that the leaders referred to Brain by name. At two hundred he stopped counting. 'It was ridiculous, we were sycophantic and dishonest but the truth is that we had no emotional strength to oppose Brain, even if we had been able to truly see what was going on', Williams says. Mel Lloyd was one congregation member who was deeply disturbed by what she saw. 'It was almost as if they were worshipping Chris, instead of Christ; I saw it as idolatry', she says. However, when she shared her doubts with other NOS members they were unwilling to hear what she had to say. This meeting was one of the turning points that led her to leaving NOS, the Anglican church that she realized was becoming disturbingly cult-like.

There are a number of things that need to be said about the context of the prophecy to explain its impact. First, Brain was incredibly skilled at manipulating his leaders into positions of dependency and vulnerability. Initially they were impressed by his radical, creative, egalitarian ideas and his passionate beliefs. The theology he espoused dovetailed with their disillusionment with the narrowness of their more traditional evangelical or Charismatic Christianity. He offered them a living vision for a faith that had become jaded. They were eager to know him and considered him to be prophetic in his far-reaching ideas for Christianity.

Brain gradually manipulated them into positions of vulnerability in which they would 'confess' their weaknesses and fears. Subtly and over time, he would nurture neuroses about these weaknesses, playing on individuals' sense of inner isolation (thereby increasing it) and he would begin to offer himself as the solution. Once a dependency was created, Brain would become progressively more abusive, and by this time the leaders were not in a position to oppose him. The truth is that Brain maintained an equilibrium between offering people 'solutions' and hope and treating them abusively, and this held people in a destructive tension.

That is not to say that Brain was not sincere in his prophecies. Williams believes that Brain was initially genuine in his intentions and became progressively corrupted by power during the life of the Nine O'clock Service. But the dramatic effect of the prophecies on the leaders is explained not only by Brain's domineering, astute and manipulative relationships with them. The leaders have pointed out that Brain gained a great deal of his power from the Charismatic theology that enabled him to say 'I have prayed a great deal about this and God says' . . . The Charismatic culture enabled Brain to prophesy in damaging ways to individuals and to groups.

In effect these prophecies became a controlling technique on the group of leaders. On one occasion a leader fell out with Brain and left, and Brain, using archetypal spiritual warfare language, told the others that the devil would be making sure the defector paid for his faithlessness. 'We were told that this leader would be given a hard time by the devil because the protecting "hedge" of the Holy Spirit would be removed because he was not in God's will', Williams recalls. He adds, 'It was not just that Chris was a damaging personality; he leaned heavily on Charismatic theology and prophecy in particular, when he made these statements.' The other leaders were led to believe that 'stepping out of God's will' would lead to their life being ruined. Brain was seen as the purveyor of God's will and hence, there was considerable pressure to obey him and to support his ideas.

Williams describes a situation in which Brain returned from staying with John Wimber and some of the Kansas City Prophets in California, and used one of the prophecies that had been given to attack his leaders. He had been told that a swarm of hornets was surrounding his head and that this represented evil. He interpreted the hornets as his leaders, telling them that unless they 'sorted themselves out', then the Sword of Damocles would come down and kill them. 'Some leaders were actually scared that unless they faced their own inner problems and conquered them, then they would die', Williams recalls. The effect of this was increased neuroses and increased loyalty to Brain.

Another group who were corporately affected by Brain's prophecies were the Homebase Team. This was a group of women who in the later years of the Nine O'clock Service became 'servants' (they were also described as post-modern nuns) for Brain, to allow him to pursue his ministry. They were not allowed to talk about their work to other members of the congregation, and their stories reveal a harrowing mixture of sexual manipulation and psychological abuse at the hands of

Brain. Williams remembers Brain describing a 'prophetic' picture of a 'Whore-Nun'. 'He described a nun who was an image of innocence and purity changing into a rotten, putrid, lascivious prostitute. The idea was that members of the Homebase Team were becoming distorted from their original purpose of serving God through helping Brain and his wife around the house, by their sexual and emotional desire for Brain; he thought that they were becoming whore-like.'

Brain spoke to members of the Homebase Team about this and told them to sort out their motives and priorities. Yet Williams feels that this 'prophecy' was a way for Brain to project the blame for the sexual misconduct between Brain and the Homebase Team onto the women. The women may have dressed provocatively, but this, he says, was because Brain demanded that they do so. They may have been over-awed or infatuated with Brain, but this was because he encouraged this and worked hard at manipulating them and creating dependency. Although this prophecy may have reflected tensions and dilemmas within Brain, Williams feels that it was pure manipulation. A number of women approached Williams about this prophecy and its interpretation. He says, 'They were distressed and humiliated, but ultimately it was simply a control mechanism that Brain used.'

So how did 'prophecy' affect the Nine O'clock Service as a whole? The public prophecies were much less dogmatic and dictatorial and largely affected the service in terms of the theological direction or new ventures. However, the controlling and domineering nature of Brain's prophecies to smaller groups (in particular the leaders) had an effect on the whole congregation. Williams believed that the damaging impact of these 'prophecies' (and the abusive, authoritarian power structures) was lessened because the extremes were filtered out by the leaders close to Brain. They generally did not have the confidence to prophesy with such force and authority, and they found (to varying degrees) abusing people unnatural. He concedes, however, that the whole culture of the Nine O'clock Service was highly controlling and abusive and that this obviously 'trickled down' from Brain and the core leaders, of which Williams was one. Williams concludes, 'We had "reflected authority" which allowed us to control others but prophetic insight was a crucial factor in his more extreme controlling behaviours; it gave him the Divine mandate to get power, and it was power that destroyed him as a leader and went on to destroy the Nine O'clock Service.'

Notes

1. R. Howard interview with Morris Cerullo, *Time Out*, August 1993.

2. R. Howard interview with Morris Cerullo, *The Observer*, Summer 1993.

Words of Knowledge, Words of Fear

It's a bitterly cold evening in a large Gothic country house just outside Lancaster. The wind is unruly, battering the thick stone walls. Following an afternoon in which the rain came down with a vengeance, darkness falls. Inside the house, in a large, plush, high-ceilinged room, fifty or so people are oblivious to the world outside. With arms aloft, voices raised, and eyes pressed tightly closed with some inner intensity, they are pouring out their souls to their Maker. The music group at the front are pumping out rhythmic and strident songs: 'Jesus is Lord, Jesus is Lord', the audience sing over and over. This is serious commitment. As the rhythm ebbs, people raise their faces heavenward, singing in tongues and praying; there is a peaceful glaze, a blissful simplicity, a warm uniformity about their expressions. The music group at the front create a soothing background as they improvise a mellifluous sequence of minor chords; prayer and singing in tongues now take centre stage.

'The Lord is saying that there are people here who have been involved in freemasonry', says Clive Corfield, the leader, eyes closed in an expression of intense concentration. The atmosphere thickens as prayer becomes more fervent but no one responds. Minutes later he continues: 'It could be that their relatives or ancestors were involved and that the spirits have been passed down the ancestral line.' By now there are five or six on their feet, surrounded by participants and helpers. They pray quietly in tongues with their hands over the heads of those being prayed for.

Twenty minutes later the leader believes that God is telling him that there are people who have 'ungodly sexual soul ties'. 'The act of intercourse outside marriage leads to ungodly soul ties which can allow demons to enter', he explains. Several respond to the prophecy by going to the front. 'I take control of every demonic power', says the leader as helpers surround those receiving ministry. Every so often the helpers ask if God is saying anything. Other helpers gently suggest what they feel that God might be saying. Some of those being prayed for start twitching, coughing, hyper-ventilating or shaking (called 'manifesting'), and others collapse on the floor.

Ten minutes later God gives the leader a picture of a cartoon character on a rock in the sea being continually pounded by the waves. The leader interprets this as meaning that there are people in the room (he describes them as weary warriors) who are exhausted, who are at the end of their tether after giving to others in their ministry. 'If this applies to you come to the front', he says. The majority of participants go forward, the helpers or counsellors move in to minister, the music soothes the ragged edges of overwrought psyches and soon several have collapsed, 'slain in the Spirit', into the arms of waiting counsellors. Some writhe on the floor, surrounded by benign, smiling helpers.

The scene is a Deliverance Ministry Training Course at Ellel Grange, near Lancaster, an independent centre specializing in healing and deliverance. Thirty people have paid £114 for a four day course to learn how to carry out exorcisms (these days known as deliverance), and all afternoon there has been a growing apprehension at the discovery that central to the course is an evening ministry session where they themselves are delivered of their own demons. They have spent the afternoon 'relaxing', chatting with other participants and filling out forms. The forms, however, are unusual. One is a family tree on an A4 sheet. The idea is to trace as much as is known about parents, grandparents and beyond if possible, to locate possible demons that might have travelled down the generational line. There is a special box to fill in on one's marriage partner in case one has picked up any demons from him or her. The other form is a questionnaire of several pages. From the questionnaire it becomes apparent that there are literally hundreds of ways of becoming possessed, or 'demonized', as the Ellel leaders call it. Alternative medicine, the New Age, traffic accidents, miscarriages, smoking, masturbation and just about any sexual position bar the missionary position can lead to demonization; or any of your relatives or ancestors being involved in these things. These forms are to enable participants to be sensitive to inner prompting or prophecies from the leadership or 'counselling' team, concerning demons that may arise during the ministry session.

The next morning members of the course are asked to 'testify', to share with the group about what had happened to them during the ministry session. Almost immediately a computer programmer raises his hand. He explains that he stood up in response to yesterday's prophecy about people being involved with freemasonry. He had no involvement and to the best of his knowledge nobody in his family had been involved either, but he stood up 'just in case'. Since he had started 'manifesting signs of demonization', by shaking, and had ended up being exorcized on the floor, he realized that, in fact, people in his family must have been masons without his knowing, perhaps some way down the 'generational line'.

A man in his late fifties says that he responded to a prophecy concerning repressed anger. The night before, he collapsed into a young man's arms during prayer. He started groaning and struggling with those praying over him, and was taken into a corner for ministry. Throughout the evening, long after the other participants had left the room, he could be heard screaming, snorting and crying out. About five hours later, with a little help from Ellel's leaders, counsellors and his wife, the final demons were despatched. It was nearly midnight. Next morning, looking shaken and tired, he testified: it had been good for him, he said.

These 'prophecies' might have done no discernible harm to those involved, but watching such experiences does lead one to question the authority of such 'prophecy'. Surely the young man's supposed connection with freemasonry (quite apart from the highly tendentious suggestion that such a connection necessitates demonic possession!) was imagined, a case of autosuggestion in a particularly open man in a highly suggestible state. As an observer of the scene, my impression was that this suggestibility was such that he started 'manifesting'; it did not seem that he was pretending, it seemed that he was he was in an emotional state which rendered him open to almost anything. In the epistles Paul wrote of testing prophecy; how do these Bible believing Christians do this?

According to the Bishop Dominic Walker, the Church of England's Chief Adviser on Healing and Deliverance, there is a danger that preachers, by making general prophecies to large audiences, encourage vulnerable and suggestible individuals to respond. He says, 'Once individuals respond and approach the

Minister they are particularly open to the Minister's agenda. The agenda may be Satanic abuse, sexual abuse, abortion or the occult, but it is likely that his views will be forceful and it is quite possible for the Minister's bête noire to be projected onto the victim.'

Dr Bill Thompson, a lecturer in Sociology at Reading University, says that this is exactly what happened in the spate of Satanic abuse horror stories in the early 1990s. Although these cases did not involve 'prophecy' in the counselling situation, Ministers and church workers, with the best intentions, led the victims towards their agenda. Thomson explains: 'It was almost as if the Minister's own problems, or objects of hate, became transferred. You rarely had Satanic abuse mentioned without a Charismatic Christian, convinced that there are hordes of Satanists waiting to eat your baby.' He points to Maureen Davies, formerly of Reachout Trust (a Christian organization set up to help people to come out of occult activities) who in her counselling claimed to have come across several cases of Satanic abuse, but who, in a BBC Wales investigation in 1991, did not take the opportunity to substantiate any of the cases investigated. Thomson believes her committed belief in Satanic abuse may have convinced some of her counsellees that they had been involved in it.

Thomson believes that there is much greater danger with 'prophecy'. He says: 'These things were happening in "relatively rational" counselling sessions; anything could happen in the subjective realm of prophecy. The Minister's subconscious has an "access all areas" pass which could have frightening consequences for the person involved.' Thomson believes that such 'prophecy' is potentially dangerous and could quite easily lead to 'victims' experiencing false memory syndrome – in which counsellors or priests inadvertently implant 'memories' into their clients during counselling or ministry. What is particularly worrying is that there is little accountability in the area. Many new church leaders are accountable to no-one; even Anglicans have a loose pastoral structure which allows vicars to ignore a bishop's advice, explaining that they are answerable only to God.

Apart from the possibility of being misled there are potential psychological problems for the recipient of a 'prophecy' too. Once the 'prophecy' is given to the counsellee it is often directive and demands a response. According to Dominic Walker: 'If someone is told that God is saying that they have been sexually abused, the onus is on them to respond.' To react by rejecting the 'word of knowledge' of the prophet (invariably a person in authority and held in respect) is difficult and may seem to the counsellee as though they are rejecting their faith. Walker adds: 'The temptation to go along with the prophecy rather than face the conflict with the counsellor/prophet must be great.'

Such people are usually with the preacher or counsellor because they are in some way seeking help and are unable to cope alone. To expect them to reject the prophecy is in many cases unrealistic; it would involve dilemmas (if the counsellee trusts the preacher, can they cope with them, or their God, being wrong) and necessitate considerable emotional strength and balance. Walker believes that prophecy is something which should have absolutely no part in counselling, and adds that counsellors should be seeking to help people to find their own solutions rather than propagating their own agenda.

According to David Altman, Chairman of the Association of Christian Counsellors Training Committee, a large part of the problem is a blurring of the edges between counselling and Charismatic ministry (involving prayer, laying on of hands and prophecy). 'Prophecy should not occur in a counselling situation', he says, 'it is a ministry to be used in a completely different context.' He stresses that the Association of Christian Counsellors write clear and strict contracts between counsellees and counsellors and that ACC's guidelines are the same as those of the British Association for Counselling. Altman admits, however, that in practice Christian counsellors (ACC affiliated and others) may well give prophecies, particularly if the counselling takes place in a church setting. 'Unfortunately, it does happen and far too often. I live in fear of the "You were abused by your parents" type of prophecy,' he adds. The Evangelical Alliance have expressed 'fears that some Christian counsellors are unintentionally harming people who come to them.' They are particularly concerned about 'word of knowledge' (prophecy) being used in a counselling situation and are producing guidelines for churches.

Dr Andrew Fergusson, General Secretary of the Christian Medical Fellowship, says 'There is an urgent need for churches to develop strict guidelines and safeguards in sensitive areas of counselling. If this does not happen further pastoral damage will be done.' However, as Altman says: 'This whole area is very hard to regulate. All we can do is offer good guidelines based on professional practice and offer help to those who have had bad experiences at the hands of naïve but harmful counsellors.' He admits that the whole area is dangerously subjective and that the prophecies may well say more about the prophet (and his or her subconscious) than they do about the counsellee.

Rebecca Dallimore, a well balanced 21 year old with learning difficulties who had attended a special school, was sitting in her back garden hitting herself with stones. She had been unusually quiet recently but her parents, David and Valerie Dallimore, had put it down to sadness at her grandmother's recent death. Mrs Dallimore left the kitchen to hang out the washing and saw Rebecca hitting herself. Rebecca had never deliberately abused herself before and Mrs Dallimore thought little of it but told her to stop. She said jokingly: 'What are you doing? You'll be locked up if you go around doing things like that.' These words proved (in the secular sense) prophetic, and the shock waves of future events were to lead to the Dallimores losing their daughter and to an acrimonious battle centring on the village church and splitting the community. Unknown to the Dallimores, they were dealing with sinister powers and beliefs that they had no understanding or knowledge of. They were out of their depth.

The Dallimore family, David, Val, Rebecca and their other children, Andrew and Theresa, had moved to the sleepy Norfolk village of Hockwold-cum-Wilton a year and a half earlier. Ironically, they had moved for Rebecca's protection and peace of mind. In their former town, Addlestone in Surrey, Rebecca had had some traumatic experiences that they were all keen to put behind her. 'We thought a fresh start would be good and decided that living in a small rural village would help her recover', Mrs Dallimore says. The Dallimores gave up their jobs, sold their house and bought a bungalow in Hockwold-cum-Wilton. 'It seemed the ideal safe place to move to', Mrs Dallimore adds.

Initially all went well. Mrs Dallimore got a job in a local hospital, Mr Dallimore worked unloading lorries at a depot in Thetford. Rebecca was much more stable and she got a job in an old people's home. She started breeding guinea pigs and enjoyed looking after her cherished terrier, Jack. 'We thought we'd done the right thing and things were going really well, Rebecca was much happier', her mother recalls. However, when the old people's home changed its status to a residential home, Rebecca lost her job and was unemployed for several months. The death of her grandmother was also a severe blow. The whole family were shocked but Rebecca took it particularly badly. 'They had been very close. Rebecca brooded over that death, she really missed her', Mrs Dallimore explains. In the event, the most significant factor proved to be Rebecca's lack of friends. 'It's such a small village, Rebecca made friends with neighbours but she was still lonely', Mrs Dallimore says.

When Mrs Dallimore's sister came to visit she suggested that Rebecca joined the local church. The Dallimores are Catholics but since moving from Addlestone had stopped attending church because there were no local Catholic churches. The local church was St James', the Anglican parish church. 'I thought that it was a good idea at the time', Mrs Dallimore says, 'I mean what harm could come to someone going to their local C of E and making friends?' Rebecca started attending Sunday morning services, but fairly soon went to other church-based activities, such as Bible studies and the Wednesday evening healing meeting at the rectory.

After some months involved with the church, Rebecca started describing people talking in strange languages and writhing across the floor like a snake. 'Rebecca thought it was funny, but I was concerned and told her not to get involved in any of that herself', Mrs Dallimore says. 'She told me that she did not and that she thought it was silly', she continues. Mrs Dallimore was reluctant to tell her to stop going, because Rebecca seemed to be enjoying it; she had made lots of friends.

The parish worker, Jenny Roughan, was one of her friends. 'They were inseparable at one stage', Mrs Dallimore recalls, 'but it was always at the house of Jenny and Brian Roughan, we hardly saw her.' Mr Dallimore describes seeing Jenny rush up to Rebecca and hug her with unusual intensity as he dropped her off for a church meeting. A neighbour of the Dallimores and a member of St James' Parochial Church Council, was concerned at the influence of Jenny Roughan and others at the church on Rebecca. 'I could see that Rebecca was eager to please and very easily influenced and I had misgivings about what the happy clappies would do with such a person. The worst that I thought could happen was that she would become another of them', she says.

What the Dallimores, as relative newcomers, were not aware of was that the Revd Arthur Rowe had split the church because of his extreme Charismatic beliefs, and that his followers had who met at the Wednesday evening healing meetings were zealously practising spiritual gifts such as prophecy, exorcism and healing. The vicar was a figure of great controversy in the community. As early as October 1991 he claimed 'a vision of healing' was received and, as he wrote in his parish magazine in March 1993: 'We have experienced extraordinary miracles, all verifiable, including healings of: cancer, deafness, dumbness, invalidism, including MS, psoriasis, arthritis . . .' In a subsequent parish magazine Rowe claimed that a medical assessor had attended meetings, and suggested that he had confirmed the miracles. By Christmas 1993, Dr Greer, the medical assessor, wrote that the Bishop of Huntingdon had asked him to attend the meetings because he was concerned about them. Dr Greer wrote: 'I have not confirmed any healing . . . I was, however, a little anxious with some of the claims.'

Apart from his obsessive belief that he was a miracle worker, the Revd Arthur Rowe also had an interest in Satanists and demons. In January 1994, he wrote in his parish magazine that the theft of church furnishings was likely to be the work of Satanists. He wrote: 'the theft of the chairs could be allocated to antique thieves . . . but not the theft of the Altar in the Lady Chapel along with its furnishings. The latter, in particular, and probably the whole has to do with Satanic worship which is carried out within the boundaries of these villages.' On other occasions the Revd Arthur Rowe reported Satanic meetings and witches' covens to the police. They have never found any evidence to substantiate his claims. A journalist once went to investigate a 'Satanic altar' to find out that it was a hay bail.

The Revd Arthur Rowe's wild imaginings were more damaging when they concerned people. Mrs Day, one of his parishioners, attended one of his Wednesday night healing meetings when, in the middle of the meeting, Rowe said, 'You are full of the stench of Satan.' He then closed the meeting and Mrs Day was asked to leave. The next day one of Rowe's church workers, visited Mrs Day to tell her that God had told the Revd Rowe that she was possessed by the devil and to offer her an exorcism.

Mrs Day declined but has suffered nightmares since that evening.

It was at one of these Wednesday night healing meetings that the problems started for the Dallimore family. Rebecca was depressed following her grandmother's death, and after several months out of work. She had convinced herself that she had cancer, and Rowe and his supporters prayed for her and claimed another 'miraculous healing'. Then one evening it was prophesied (it is not clear by whom) that Rebecca had been Satanically abused by her parents. Rebecca immediately fell to the floor crying and was 'ministered to' and counselled by those in attendance. It was assumed that the prophecy had been accurate.

Meanwhile the Dallimores were pleased that Rebecca's social life had taken a turn for the better. 'We were pleased that she got out and saw people', says Mrs Dallimore, 'we had no idea about what was going on.' Following the prophecy, Rebecca started describing outlandish and lurid stories of Satanic rituals with her parents. Each time this happened the Revd Arthur Rowe and his followers were all too keen to accept Rebecca's stories as true. Rebecca described being raped by her father in a Satanic ritual on the kitchen table, being forced to kiss her grandmother in another ritual at her grandmother's funeral. She told of seventeen years of Satanic abuse within her family. It was at this stage that Mrs Dallimore found Rebecca in the garden hitting herself with stones. 'The conflict within her must have been so great as she tried to please her new friends and went along with the prophecy', Mrs Dallimore explains, 'while all the time realizing that she was making it up.'

About six weeks after the first prophecy, Rebecca told her parents that she was going away with friends for the weekend. The Dallimores were pleased, remarking how Rebecca was more active socially. In fact Rebecca was being taken into hiding by members of the church, convinced that Rebecca was frequently being abused in Satanic ceremonies and wanting to rescue her. A few days later Rebecca 'phoned to say that she was not coming home and that she had got a job. 'She didn't sound normal', Mrs Dallimore says, 'I could tell that there was something wrong, but she wouldn't tell me.' Mrs Dallimore tried to find out where Rebecca was and 'phoned her friends from church.

She was directed to the house of some of Revd Rowe's most

zealous supporters. When the Dallimores arrived and knocked on the door they heard Rebecca inside screaming, 'Go away, go away, I don't want to see you! I hate you!' When the door was opened the Dallimores asked what was going on. Other supporters of Rowe arrived, and one started behaving aggressively, saying: 'We don't like rapists and child abusers round here.' Mrs Dallimore intervened before a fight started. 'David couldn't believe it, he was really angry and this so-called Christian was spoiling for a fight', Mrs Dallimore recalls.

In the subsequent confrontation the Dallimores realized that the church had taken Rebecca into hiding and that Rebecca did not want to see them. 'We didn't know what was going on, we were devastated, but what could we do?' Mrs Dallimore says. They walked home bewildered and in tears. The police explained that since Rebecca was an adult they could not help, and the Dallimores were left helpless, not knowing what had happened to their daughter and not knowing what to do.

The next day the Dallimores 'phoned friends and relatives seeking advice and support. Mrs Dallimore says, 'It was almost as if she had been kidnapped and brainwashed. We really couldn't understand what had made her so aggressive towards us, she'd always been such a warm and loving daughter.' It was only next Sunday when a neighbour attended church that things started to become clear. Arthur Rowe announced from the pulpit that the church had taken a girl into its care who had been abused for seventeen years.

After 'phoning various agencies involved in monitoring religious cults and supporting families who had 'lost' relatives to them, they came across Catalyst, an agency run by Graham Baldwin, a counsellor specializing in victims of 'religious abuse'. Baldwin, a former Pentecostal minister says: 'As soon as I met them I knew they were genuine. The whole scenario was disturbingly familiar amongst extreme Charismatic Christians who have an obsession with demons and the devil.' Mrs Dallimore had found someone familiar with the area, who was supportive and was a tenacious campaigner for victims of religious abuse.

Months later, in December 1993, the police asked the Dallimores to come to the station. They went with their solicitor and were arrested on arrival. Mr Dallimore was put in a cell and interviewed and Mrs Dallimore was driven home so that the police could search the house. 'I had nothing to hide, I just said take what you want, do what you need to', Mrs Dallimore recalls. They took videos, two crucifixes, candles and various creams, and asked if they had a devil's mask, a black tablecloth and a vibrator. Although they did not know it, Rebecca's allegations concerned ritualistic Satanic abuse. Many of her claims were clearly shown to be untrue, but Rowe was undeterred. Rowe told a most unlikely story (presumably from Rebecca) of a church member and neighbour witnessing Mr Dallimore beating Rebecca. He did not think to check its veracity. It was flatly denied by the neighbour. In fact when the police search of the Dallimore's house found nothing to substantiate the allegations, Rowe accused the Parochial Church Council of tipping the Dallimores off so that they could destroy the evidence. Members of the PCC were outraged.

The police investigation concluded that there was absolutely no evidence that any abuse, Satanic or otherwise, had occurred. Again Arthur Rowe was undeterred, saying: 'There's nothing that I don't know about Rebecca Dallimore.' Meanwhile, he had placed Rebecca at Pilsdon Manor, a Christian retreat centre in Dorset. She has 'phoned home twice, but apart from this the family have been allowed no contact with their daughter. 'She won't see us and the Church of England are not taking responsibility for the destructive actions of one of their priests', says Mrs Dallimore.

The Right Revd Gordon Roe, the Bishop of Huntingdon, has confirmed that Rowe did not follow standard procedure for such a serious situation, and that he was only made aware of it at a very late stage. However, despite the protests of PCC members, local councillors and neighbours of the Dallimores, efforts at reconciling the family have been minimal. The church has not officially admitted that the allegations of Satanic abuse are untrue. 'The church has behaved disgracefully', says Graham Baldwin. 'They seem to be covering the whole thing up in an attempt to save face. The suffering, strain and cost of this episode on the Dallimore family seems to be their last priority.'

Arthur Rowe has now resigned and left the Hockwold area, ostensibly over his disagreement with the Church of England's ordination of women priests. The parish is starting to settle down, many of the traditional believers are starting to come back to St James'. However, the Dallimore family are still without Rebecca. As Mrs Dallimore says: 'It is frightening to think that you can be accused of Satanic abuse based on someone's prophecy in a healing meeting. That prophecy has lost us our daughter and we really want her back. We have almost lost our faith over this, the strain it has put on our marriage is tremendous and there is no end in sight.'

Morris Cerullo, Miracle Man

The billboards, magazine adverts and fliers were eye-catching and controversial: A white stick and a pair of dark glasses, broken and discarded on a rough, shadowy pavement, under the legend: 'Some will see miracles for the first time'; an equally haunting and stark image of an upturned wheelchair ('Some will be moved by the power of God for the first time') and smashed hearing aid ('Some will hear the message of the Bible *clearly* for the first time' – my italics). This was the teaser advertising campaign to Morris Cerullo's Mission to London 1992. As the campaign unfolded all became clear: at Earl's Court, in late June, people could expect miracles at the hand of Cerullo, with a little help from his friend, God.

Cerullo had been coming over for years, but in 1992 his controversial and bombastic advertising campaign made the secular media sit up and take notice. For the first time this little known but brash 'faith healer' from nowhere appeared in several national newspapers. Two episodes of the BBC's religious documentary programme *Heart of the Matter* were devoted to Cerullo, his ministry and his claims of miraculous healings. At a press conference before his opening night, scores of photographers and journalists were jostling for seats. As the diminutive figure of Morris Cerullo, looking like a cross between Bob Monkhouse and an expensively attired insurance salesman, was ushered in, there was a tangible excitement. People had not come across this type of grand American style evangelist before. As Cerullo began speaking it became clear that this was not the sedate, polite and succinct style of Billy Graham.

Cerullo was brash, confrontational and bold; he outfaced their cynicism with smiles and unashamedly grand claims. God was the miracle worker, not Morris, he stressed, referring to himself in the third person. There were no guarantees, but clearly he was expecting miracles as he had urged his followers to do. He harangued the press for their cynicism and although he was asked questions, it was evident that the press were bemused.

They did not know how to respond to this home-grown, ingenuous confidence; they had never expected such American, showy bravura to cross the Atlantic.

Disabled people were the first to react. They daubed his posters with 'Rights not Miracles' slogans, they picketed his rallies and they complained to the Advertising Standards Authority about his Mission to London campaign. One disabled persons' group circulated a letter saying: 'He is exploiting disabled people by offering miracles that we do not want and that he cannot deliver.' Ann McFarlane, a disabled Christian, said that the campaign made her feel ill: 'They are telling disabled people, you are unacceptable as you are and nobody wants you and neither does God. I believe in a Christian God who made me as I am. These posters are saying that if you cannot achieve physical perfection then you are an outcast.'

Although the ability to perform healing miracles had been central to the Charismatic's agenda since the very beginnings of the movement, it had never before been thrust into the nation's consciousness quite as rudely as it had during Cerullo's Mission to London in 1992. The gift of healing and the ministry of healing had been fundamental Charismatic beliefs and practices in thousands of churches throughout Britain, but it took the brash, showy 'in your face' style of Cerullo and his advertising campaign to make the nation take note. Miracles (or lack of miracles) were being talked about, or sneered at, for the first time.

But did the miracles happen? Did the blind see, the deaf hear and the lame dance? In short, did Cerullo deliver? Did he live up to his advertising hype? To attempt to answer this, probably the first thing to do is to define a miracle. This may seem obvious and unnecessary, but it is particularly important since in this area goal posts can move, and diagnoses tend to shift or even vaporize. The classic definition of a healing miracle comes from Lourdes, and the criteria were devised by Cardinal Lambertini in 1735, who later became Pope Benedict XIV. In *Lourdes Cures and their Medical Assessment* (by Dr St John Dowling, MA, MB, FRCGP) the rules are clearly stated:

1. The disease must be serious, incurable and unlikely to respond to treatment.

2. The disease which disappeared must not have

reached a stage at which it would have resolved by
itself.

3. No medication should have been given, or if some
   medicines were prescribed, then they must have
   had only unimportant effects. (It is most unusual
   nowadays to find a case completely untreated, and
   this rule is interpreted as excluding any patient
   who has had potentially curative treatment unless
   that treatment can be demonstrated to have
   failed.)

4. The cure must be sudden and reached instanta-
   neously. (This is now extended to include cures
   developing over a period of days.)

5. The cure must be complete, not partial or incom-
   plete.

With such rigorous criteria (not accepted by Cerullo), miracles
would appear to be relatively easy to prove or disprove. Indeed,
the veracity of Cerullo's claims of miracles was thrown into sharp
focus when the UK media started to challenge Cerullo over his
claims. In an ITN interview, Dr Peter May, a member of the
Christian Medical Fellowship, publicly challenged Cerullo over
his claims. Although Cerullo's 1993 advertising stated that 2250
people had been healed in the 1992 mission, the survey
conducted by his own organization Morris Cerullo World Evangelism, said that 476 had claimed to be healed. The
documentary programme *Heart of the Matter* followed this up by
asking Cerullo to submit the 'best' three miracles from his
mission the previous year, to medical scrutiny. Cerullo agreed
and, weeks later, presented his best nine cases. Of the nine 'best
cases' only six had allowed access to their medical notes for independent scrutiny.

Although he was not blind, three year old Azam Anjum was
presumably considered to be one of those who did 'see miracles
for the first time'. Weeks before the mission his health visitor
noted a possible squint at a routine health test. He was found to
have a lazy left eye due to longsightedness and astigmatism. The
initial test suggested that he had extremely weak vision in this
eye. Following the mission a better result was obtained for his

left eye, which Azam's mother interpreted as miraculous. Yet his optician thought that the problem remained and that the improvement was because he was less tired. After the mission, his optician told his parents that unless he wore his eye patch over his good eye, he was in danger of losing his vision in his left eye completely. His parents agreed to letting him wear his glasses again, and he has made good progress but needs stronger lenses in both eyes. Clearly Azam's 'miracle' did nothing to improve his eyesight. Despite this, one of Cerullo's subsequent leaflets suggested that Azam is now able to see clearly out of both eyes.

This readiness to claim premature miraculous healings with no substantive evidence is not limited to the medically ignorant. Dr James Muir, one of the members of Cerullo's handpicked medical panel, claimed that he had been healed of hay fever. Did he not stop to consider the pollen count or the fact that at the end of June (when his 'healing' occurred) the hay fever season is nearing its end? Somewhat unremarkably, hay fever symptoms recurred the next year and Dr Muir took medication to alleviate the condition.

One of Cerullo's best cases of someone 'moved by the power of God for the first time' was 26 year old Arlene Braham. Braham claimed to have been offered surgery after a nine year history of knee pain. When her doctor was approached, he said that he had seen her over a year ago concerning pains in the knee and had sent her to an orthopedic surgeon. Following X-rays the surgeon concluded that there were no clinical abnormalities but noted signs of a worn knee cartilage. Her GP later told her that there was nothing significantly wrong with her and that surgery was inappropriate. Arlene's 'miracle' was that her knees were basically healthy . . . before and after Mission to London 1992.

It is not unknown for Cerullo's miracle claims to evaporate once it is clear that the recipient never had the condition in the first place. Georgine McHale, a 46 year old woman and one of Cerullo's best 'cases', claimed to have been miraculously healed of a fibroid. Morris Cerullo World Evangelism (MCWE) backed this up, saying, 'Her testimony is very strong and all docum-ented.' One wonders how they attempted to verify it. In fact in April 1992, according to her doctor, she had come to him with heavy periods. Her notes have no suggestion of a fibroid being present but an ultrasound test was arranged to check this. After the mission the ultrasound confirmed that she had no fibroid, and Georgine interpreted this as miraculous.

Gloria Malcolm's case has similarities. Cerullo used her 'healing' in his advertising for Mission to London 1993, under the legend: 'Healed of a partially collapsed lung.' Underneath this Gloria Malcolm is quoted saying: 'After experiencing severe pain in my chest I was diagnosed as having a partially collapsed lung. At Mission to London, after I had called out to God for my healing, Morris Cerullo said that people with collapsed lungs were being healed by the power of God. As he said this I started to experience a burning sensation in my back. I knew that God had healed me then. My doctor confirmed that my lung was back to normal.' In fact, Dr Soole, a member of Cerullo's Medical Review Group, says that the group concluded that there was insufficient evidence to claim a miracle. He recalls that Gloria's lung showed no evidence of having collapsed. A chest X-ray had shown that she had some consolidation in her lung of the sort that would frequently follow infection in the lung. He wrote to MCWE to point out that 'further medical inform-ation was required' concerning Gloria Malcolm's case. Despite the fact that the MCWE were made aware of this in June 1993, they continued to use the advertisement in August prior to the mission.

Having been presented with Cerullo's best cases and been singularly unimpressed, *Heart of the Matter* and several national newspapers were damning in their conclusions, suggesting that the idea of miracles was fanciful, and that MCWE's presentation of facts was at times misleading. Cerullo responded combatively in a press release in which he said of *Heart of the Matter*: 'I would give the programme low water marks on the integrity of televi-sion journalism; on a scale of 1 to 10, I would have rated it a 2 . . . HOTM fell into a rut of skepticism and bias. With that in mind HOTM projected their own prejudices and refused to uphold the unsolicited testimonies of sincere persons as true, while attempting to cast doubt on their biblically-based Christian experience.' Cerullo continued by rejecting *Heart of the Matter*'s criteria for a miracle (which were less strict than the Lourdes criteria): 'HOTM's presupposition that the ultimate basis for establishing the veracity of a miracle is decided by the OPINION put forward by one medical professional is intellectually flawed and completely unreasonable.'

Cerullo also announced the establishment of a Christian medical symposium to meet in 1993, made up of Christian doctors and leaders from across the denominations and from around the world. The press release stated that the symposium will 'put forward the subject of divine healing and provide irrefutable documentation of case histories, including many significant miraculous healings from Mission to London.'

This symposium, which later metamorphosed itself into a 'healing conference', took place in July 1993. Cerullo's publicity said that 450 doctors and church leaders were present, but omitted to say that only six or seven of the 450 were doctors and that some who had been critical of Cerullo's claims were excluded. In fact, prior to the symposium, a medical review group had been formed to look at the cases of supposed miracles during the 1992 mission. However, according to Dr M. J. Soole, a member of the medical review group, only three cases were discussed in detail, and there were a number of problems in producing 'irrefutable documentation' of a miracle.

The terms of reference changed; rather than aiming to produce proof of a miracle, it became more amorphous. 'Divine healing', which Dr Soole felt could refer to God's sovereignty over normal healing processes, had replaced the term 'miraculous healing.' The definition of a miracle was also unclear since the Lourdes criteria were considered too strict. Members of the medical review group seemed intent on interpreting events as miracles regardless of the evidence. As Dr Soole stated in his report on the medical review group: 'Objective evidence of medical cure was considered by many as less important than an individual assertion that a healing had occurred.' He continued: 'Indeed, it was argued by some that this affirmation was true even if the medical evidence argued otherwise. In such cases, the individual concerned had been healed, but waited "in faith" to experience their healing.' Soole's conclusion was that 'none of the cases discussed lies outside the realm of normal clinical experience and, as such, provides no grounds for claiming "irrefutable evidence of miraculous healing".'

This dogged insistence on miracles having occurred, despite the practical and medical evidence suggesting otherwise, is one of the most worrying aspects of Cerullo's supposed miracles.

Janet Nwata, a health visitor, believed that she had been healed of poor eyesight and consequently threw away her glasses. Her testimony appeared in Cerullo's publicity material: 'My eyesight was very bad. On the Wednesday evening of Mission to London, I felt like scales were falling from my eyes. Since then I have been able to read and write perfectly without my glasses on.' However, six weeks later she started getting severe headaches. Her optician subsequently informed her that her eyesight had deteriorated and recommended stronger glasses. Nwata reported this to MCWE and was told that she had to pray harder to claim her healing. She was disappointed and upset but nevertheless was determined to return to Cerullo's next mission to claim her miracle.

Temitope, a young girl, is a more worrying case of one of Cerullo's followers believing that a miracle has occurred and not facing the possibility that it has not. Following the mission, her parents insisted that her poor eyesight had been healed and insisted on taking her unusually thick glasses away from her. Temitope's parents refused to allow an independent doctor to arrange an eye test and would not let her have her glasses back, despite the fact that she requested them.

A severe case of damage following an irrational and determined insistence that a miracle had occurred, concerns a 25 year old with a relatively minor ailment. Audrey Reynolds attended Mission to London 1992 and was convinced that she had been miraculously healed of an ankle injury. She was convinced that she had been completely healed and stopped taking all medication, including her drugs for epilepsy. Six days after her 'miracle' she had an epileptic seizure in the bath and drowned. The Southwark Coroner, Sir Montague Levine, concluded: 'It is a tragedy that she went to this meeting and thought she had been cured of everything. Sadly it led to her death.'

The head in the sand approach of participants in healing meetings is almost as remarkable as the spurious and misleading claims of healing itself. Dr Peter May, who is one of Cerullo's severest critics, as well as being a committed Christian and 'miracle buster', believes that the credulousness of recipients of divine healing is shocking and potentially life threatening. He says, 'Healers have much to answer for; they appear to be exploiting vulnerable people who are desperate for a miracle.'

May has scientifically investigated scores of 'miracles' (Christian and New Age) and has yet to find one that stands up to medical scrutiny. He lays part of the blame on the healer's misleading hype, which he believes is partly wishful thinking. He adds: 'It may also be a western cultural phenomenon in which rationally bound westerners jettison their reason as a reaction to conversion in some of the more extreme religious groups.'

In India Cerullo's miracle machine met with a much more robust response. On October 17th 1993, *The Times of India* reported a mission in Calcutta that Cerullo must be keen to forget. Under the headline 'Bitter Therapy for Faith-Healer', they describe a riot when Indians decided that the healings were fake and stormed the stage. Approximately 30,000 locals gathered at a park to hear Cerullo speak, expecting miracles. MCWE had taken full page newspaper advertisements inviting people of all faiths and with all illnesses to attend, and encouraging them to expect miraculous healings. It also stated that over 200,000 people had experienced the power of God in a service in Madras. The curious, the sick and the handicapped converged on Park Circus, some arriving in ambulances and on stretchers. Cerullo spoke for nearly two hours and then proclaimed that the sick and handicapped had been cured. The sick and the handicapped and their friends and relatives were not so convinced, and according to *The Times of India* 'pandemonium broke out'. The article continues:

> As evidence, he asked a few people who had been sitting within the enclosure near the dais, to come to the dais and say that they had been healed. But members of the rationalist group and some journalists present there challenged whether those people were really deaf or dumb, or they were pretending as such to deceive the assembled crowd. Besides, the people who had accompanied the real deaf and dumb and the handicapped people began to shout that their relations had not been cured at all. The crowd became increasingly angry as Cerullo was unable to prove his healing power and started chanting, 'Go back Cerullo', before storming the platform. At this point the police moved in and rescued Cerullo and

fought back the crowd with bamboo clubs. Cerullo was arrested and interviewed, and the next morning he was declared *persona non grata* and bundled out of the country.

Interestingly, according to Tim Pain, one of Cerullo's British admirers and apologists, Cerullo told him that the Mission had been worth it, because while he was in custody Cerullo had brought the Calcutta Police Commissioner 'to the Lord'. Had Pain spoken to the Police Commissioner to confirm his conversion? He had not.

Fairytale Healing

In 1981 life was a fairytale for Jennifer Rees-Larcombe. In her late thirties all her childhood dreams had come true; life was heavenly. She had six healthy children, a successful husband, a cottage in the idyllic Kent countryside, ducks, chickens, even a chocolate-box golden labrador. She grew vegetables, tended her flowers, went blackberrying down leafy country lanes and wrote books. As she says on the video *Unexpected Healing*: 'It was a heavenly kind of life really. It was really as if we'd built heaven on earth.'

According to her book of the same title, *Unexpected Healing*, in the spring of 1982 her cosy and secure world was turned upside down. Despite the fact that 'Jen' was a fighter she had to admit that she was ill. She had been suffering in solitude, biting her lip and getting on with life as best as she could, when a friend called the doctor on her behalf. She had had a sore throat and a continual headache for three months and then the pain had started to go down her spine. On the morning when the doctor arrived, he wasted no time and despatched Jennifer off to the Emergency Department at Kent and Sussex Hospital. On arrival, Jennifer recalls, 'people swarmed around me, but they were all upside down from my position . . . I discovered I was able to escape from them all simply by sliding under a warm woolly blanket of sleep. Its drowsy folds became more real to me than the disturbing things that were happening in the bustling world all around me.' Reality was a frightening place for Jennifer.

In *Unexpected Healing* she says that she was diagnosed as having encephalitis (acute inflammation of the brain and the membranes that surround the brain) in 1982. Between 1984 and 1987 she had four more attacks of encephalitis. A footnote explains that encephalitis is usually a life threatening condition without any known effective treatment, adding that some people make a complete recovery. Jennifer says that all light and sound was amplified to unbearable intensity, she lost all feeling in her limbs, she suffered convulsions and could not speak. In between these attacks many of the symptoms remained, and her neurologists described this condition as myalgic encephalomyelitis or ME. On the video, Jennifer describes a 'brush with death' in which her swallowing, breathing and heartbeat stopped functioning. During this, she had an out-of-the-body experience and was given the archetypal choice by the archetypal benign divine presence: heaven or bedlam? By the skin of her teeth she opted for going back to uncomfortable reality. 'I suppose they resuscitated me', she says, adding that she almost immediately felt pangs of regret.

Jennifer was moved to a hospital in London for further tests. She had brain scans, X-rays and an electroencephalogram. In London Jennifer explained to a doctor that she had had encephalitis before, and she asked why it was taking so long for her to recover. She was told that she had developed a complication: her nerve casings had become inflamed. Not surprisingly, at one stage Jennifer became seriously depressed and considered taking an overdose of sleeping pills. Some time later she was put in a wheelchair to be taken back to the Kent and Sussex Hospital. On the traumatic wheelchair journey out of the hospital, Jennifer recalls, 'suddenly I felt Christ himself was right there in that concrete corridor, experiencing the pain, fear and humiliation with me. He knew from experience what it was like. He seemed to care what happened to me in this lowest moment of my life, even if no one else did.'

After two months in the Kent and Sussex, Jennifer was moved to Burrswood, a Christian nursing and convalescence centre. Four weeks later her condition was considered stable enough for her to return home. It was not, however, to be the beginning of her recovery. When she returned home, following one or two overambitious attempts to go back to normal, she realized that she was, as she says, a cripple. She still could not control her limbs, and her bowels and bladder were also proving hard to regulate. Her children were showing signs of disturbed behaviour and a neurologist told her that she was not going to get better.

By 1984 the Larcombes had moved from their cottage to a townhouse in Tunbridge Wells, to make access to doctors and social services easier. Jennifer, now frequently confined to a wheelchair, had been awarded a mobility and a severe disability allowance. She scoured the country for Christians with a gift of healing, but each time was left disappointed and wheelchair-bound. With what appears to be an indomitable fighting spirit, Jennifer started writing children's books and a Christian book about accepting disability, entitled *Beyond Healing*. Jennifer then started talking to Christians about suffering and about coming to terms with it. It was in March 1990 that Jennifer was, once again, unsettled. She thought God was saying that he wanted to heal her, but after so many hopes dashed in the past, she was reluctant to accept this and told no one of her inklings.

This feeling persisted for months, and on June 14th, while speaking on suffering at a Christian meeting in Guildford, a young woman approached her and told her that God wanted to heal her. Later on in the meeting Jennifer became convinced that she should ask the young woman to pray for her. She forced her way through the people in the church hall, propelling herself as fast as she could go in her wheelchair, desperate to catch her. She did, and the woman, a recent convert, prayed for Jennifer to be miraculously healed. Jennifer stood up straight and ran to the toilet. The members at the meeting were aghast.

On returning home that evening Jennifer's husband was equally dumbfounded as he met her walking up their front door steps, dragging the wheelchair behind her. During the next couple of weeks the Larcombes seemed to be suffering from post-miracle stress disorder. There was Jennifer making cakes, decorating the house ready for a birthday party, and taking her husband on route marches across the countryside at breakneck speed. They could not quite believe that their 'cripple' had been miraculously healed instantly at the end of a Christian meeting. As Jennifer says, God had 'turned it all round for good', He had 'made something good out of a complete failure'.

Unfortunately for the Larcombes, Dr Peter 'Miracle Buster' May could not quite believe it either. It was months later when he first heard of Jennifer's instantaneous miracle, as it started to surface in the secular and Christian press towards the end of 1990. As a Christian doctor and member of the Christian Medical Fellowship and Church of England General Synod, May found that he was frequently asked for his opinion on so-called miracles in the Charismatic wing of the church. Dr May was somewhat perplexed about Jennifer Rees-Larcombe's miracle: apparently this was a dramatic miracle in the heart of the respectable home counties. This was not American hype or hard-sell of the sort that May had investigated before; it had happened to an intelligent, mature and reasonable woman who had no obvious motives for wanting to attract attention to herself or her apparent healing (Larcombe generally avoids the term 'miracle').

Dr May arranged to meet Jennifer with a neurologist colleague of his, to try to clarify what Jennifer's illness had been. At the meeting he gleaned little information apart from Jennifer's subjective memories of her illness, some of which seemed medically unlikely. She claimed that she had suffered recurrent attacks of viral encephalitis, which Dr May knew from medical experience to be virtually unheard of. Viruses do not come back, as the body develops its immunity once it has been affected by a virus. Only a patient whose immune system had broken down with AIDS would have recurrences of viruses. This seemed unlikely. However, at the meeting, Jennifer signed a document allowing Dr May access to her medical records so that he could clarify what her official diagnosis was.

Days later a letter came from Jennifer's husband, Antony Larcombe, in which he thanked Dr May for spending time with Jennifer and stated that he shared Dr May's concern that 'in these matters it is the truth that is sought'. He added: 'I understand that Jennifer has signed a letter giving her permission for you to consult her medical records wherever these may be found. It seems perfectly appropriate that this should be done.' However, he continued by explaining that because Jennifer needed time to settle back into normal family life, he felt that it was important that she avoided publicity. Out of a desire to help Jennifer avoid the limelight, he stated that he was unwilling to allow the records to be released for 12 months.

May felt a certain amount of chagrin at this response because it seemed clear to him that Jennifer was encouraging publicity. He did not know that she was writing a book (*Unexpected Healing*) about her instantaneous recovery, but was aware that she was speaking to Christian groups about her healing and had written several magazine articles about it. She had also appeared on the front cover of *Renewal* magazine, holding her wheelchair above her head beside the legend: 'Jennifer Rees-Larcombe: Out of the Wheelchair, Walking, Leaping and Praising God'. May wrote back asking Antony Larcombe if an 'interim statement' from her doctor, stating her diagnosis and on what basis it was formed, might be possible.

When Antony Larcombe refused Dr May became suspicious. 'I could not understand why a simple statement could not be made; I did not want full medical records, just an official statement saying what the illness that she had been healed from was', May says. Equally perplexing for May was the fact that many of the Christians involved in Jennifer's case refused to help him and urged him to discontinue his inquiries. Dr Gareth Tuckwell, Director of Burrswood healing centre (where Jennifer had spent a considerable amount of time), would not ask Jennifer if she would cooperate with May, and suggested that it did not actually matter whether what had occurred was a miracle or a natural, scientifically explicable healing. May wrote to Dr Tuckwood stressing that it was important to verify the scientific facts, because others would ask themselves why Jennifer had been healed and not them.

He wrote: 'The several neurologists she has seen must have come to conclusions of a sort. Are they in agreement? What were the results of brain scans, lumbar punctures and electro-encephalograms?' He continued: 'What if all the results were normal and their agreed opinion was that she was an hysteric? Not unknown in the medical world, I am sure you agree, and there are a number of clues in her book which would fit that description.' Dr Tuckwell responded by restating his position while shedding more light on his motives: 'Focusing on scientific proof in the area of miraculous cure can, I believe, become a real stumbling block to faith, limit our ministry and limit our God to our own understanding.'

In June 1991, nine months after his original request to see Jennifer's medical records, Dr May asked Antony Larcombe if Jennifer's original permission might be honoured, or, if that was not possible, if a doctor's statement of her neurological diagnosis could be released. Jennifer responded by thanking May for his patience, and saying that when she had given permission for him to have access to her medical records she had felt pressurized. She concluded 'that such research would be both dishonouring to God and embarrassing to my doctors'.

May exercised his patience once again and asked for a simple statement of diagnosis to clarify exactly what her illness was. Jennifer's next letter-cum-homily gave May another opportunity to cultivate his patience. She wrote: 'I now see that my refusal to let you investigate my medical records has led you to believe that I am hiding something or that some of my doctors felt my illness was all in the mind. I assure you there was never any question of this.' In case May was not sufficiently assured, Jennifer continued: 'There is nothing there that I am ashamed of and would not be willing to have made public.' Nevertheless, Jennifer was not willing to make it public. She concluded icily with a suggestion: 'I expect you will be glad to return to your evangelistic work now that your investigation for the synod is completed.'

May believes he eventually got access to Jennifer's medical records by accident. She sent him a copy of *Unexpected Healing*, with an accompanying letter saying casually that he could check anything that he was unhappy about with her GP. May sent the letter alongside the original written permission, and requested a copy of Jennifer's medical records. He got them by return of post. 'I could not believe my luck', he says: 'After all that wrangling I received all her medical records, not just a diagnostic statement of her illness.' What May discovered was that Jennifer had never had encephalitis. Neither was there any record of epilepsy (convulsions), inflamed nerves, or of a near death experience in which she was resuscitated. During all her visits to hospitals the doctors could find nothing wrong with her physically. Her brain scans, lumbar punctures, nerve conduction studies and encephalograms showed that her condition was normal. Doctors' notes taken during her years of hospital visits state that examinations were 'singularly unrevealing', and 'predictably, on examination there are absolutely no abnormal physical findings.' She had never had a physical illness, let alone a life threatening one. The nearest she came to death was when she considered taking an overdose in the midst of her misery during her mysterious 'illness'.

The only ambiguity arises out of a clerical error in which ME (myalgic encephalomyelitis) is mistakenly described as myalgic encephalitis. It is clear that the doctor is referring to ME because he also describes it by its other name, Icelandic Disease. Although they sound similar they are completely unrelated conditions, ME having no physical manifestations. Unable to find any physical ailment, Jennifer was indeed diagnosed as having ME, a condition often linked with depression or a period of convalescence following organic illnesses. This diagnosis was held to in the absence of any objective physical findings.

The possibility that the illness may have had its origins in the mind is never stated but appears to be hinted at in Jennifer's medical notes. On one occasion a doctor notes, 'The absence of neurological signs is interesting, and I do not think that her recent pain and palpitations have any significant structural basis.' Another seems bemused that despite weakness, giddiness, slurred speech, numbness and blurred vision, 'she manages to keep going, looking after a household of ten, producing a new novel every three months, and an article every month. She does this typing fluently.' In 1984 a doctor comments: 'I have always had the feeling that there were factors other than organic disease at work here.' Jennifer, it seems, did not get seen by a psychologist.

So was Jennifer naïve or was she lying? May is circumspect: 'It wasn't naïveté and whilst I'd avoid the term lying, the whole episode suggests that there was something to hide, as I found there was.' He concedes possible confusion over terms, but adds: 'I cannot understand why she would not let me see the diagnosis if she thought the story was as she had told it.' This disingenuousness on Jennifer's part is backed up by the fact that, when she spoke in August 1992 at the Greenbelt Festival, she was challenged about the truth of her illness, and said: 'I know that I happily, willingly gave all of my records to Dr Peter May because I had nothing to hide.'

What is equally interesting to Dr May is the church's eagerness to accept that Jennifer's recovery was miraculous and their unwillingness to face the truth. 'This speaks of a church desperate for a miracle and suggests a shallowness or insecurity of outlook', he says. 'This suggestibility is surely a sign of worrying fundamentalism; above all as Christians we must have integrity and a disinterested love which faces reality. If we go the other way, we're heading for a sort of superstitious medievalism.' May suggests that those who so untiringly seek miracles may well be equally diligent in creating, perhaps unintentionally, psychosomatic illnesses. May defines an hysteric as someone whose mental and emotional needs manifest themselves in behavioural and sometimes physical ways. It is an unstable and needy personality type. He is concerned, however, that the readiness (indeed eagerness) of Charismatics to see miracles is itself hysterical, because their beliefs and their emotional needs dictate that they will see miracles, and it is this which ensures that they do see them.

The response of many evangelicals and Charismatics to May's research is also interesting. He has been caricatured as a cynic with a personal obsession about disproving miracles. In fact May was open to the possibility of 'divine healing' and, indeed, prays for the sick. However, he believes that if terms like miracle or healing are used, then doctors should investigate them rigorously. 'I'm aware of the possibility of hype and self-deception leading to spurious claims; this does Christianity no good', he says.

May has yet to find a scientifically verifiable miracle, and sectors of the Charismatic community would clearly like him to stop investigating. If this attitude is characteristic of Charismatic Christianity, it does not bode well for the future. May says, 'A Christianity which is deluding itself, clinging to a comfort blanket God, is, I believe, immature and unattractive. We have a positive contribution to make based on the nature of Jesus rather than our self-serving and comforting notions.' He adds, 'In the absence of miracles, we shouldn't be threatened by that, but should rather seek to be active in attempts to heal society and to help the poor.'

Exorcism: Casting the Mind Back

They went across the lake to the region of Gerasenes. When Jesus got out of the boat, a man with an evil spirit came from the tombs to meet him. This man lived in the tombs, and no-one could bind him anymore, not even with a chain. For he had often been chained hand and foot, but he tore the chains apart and broke the irons on his feet. No-one was strong enough to subdue him. Night and day among the tombs and in the hills he would cry out and cut himself with stones. When he saw Jesus from a distance, he ran and fell on his knees in front of him. He shouted at the top of his voice, 'What do you want with me, Jesus, Son of the Most High God? Swear to God that you won't torture me!' For Jesus had said to him, 'Come out of this man, you evil spirit!' Then Jesus asked him, 'What is your name?' 'My name is Legion', he replied, 'for we are many.' And he begged Jesus again and again not to send them out of the area.

A herd of pigs was feeding on the nearby hillside. The demons begged Jesus, 'Send us among the pigs; allow us to go into them.' He gave them permission, and the evil spirits came out and went into the pigs. The herd, about two thousand in number, rushed down the steep bank into the lake and were drowned. Those tending the pigs ran off and reported this in town and countryside, and the people went out to see what had happened. When they came to Jesus, they saw the man who had been possessed by the legion of demons, sitting there, dressed and in his right mind; and they were afraid.

Mark 5: 1–15 NIV

Exorcism has been around for a while. Indeed all cultures have their demon killers and ghostbusters, and it is fair to say that outside the Judeo-Christian framework, the rituals for despatching the malign presences or beings are often surprisingly similar. Although the devil is largely a feature of the New Testament (belief in an individual devil emerged in the late Hellenistic period of Judaism), there are isolated references to exorcism and demons in the Old Testament. Though there is only a handful of descriptions of Jesus carrying out exorcisms, the concept of demon possession was clearly more pronounced in Jesus' time. Jesus did not create belief in demons: it was in the culture around him. Just as Jesus must have believed that the world was flat, so he must have taken demon possession seriously. As Christians of all persuasions would agree, whatever else he was, he was the 'bodily Incarnation' in a historical, theological and cultural framework. He saw the world through first-century Palestine lenses.

It is possible that Jesus may have warned his followers not to get too carried away (or even obsessed) with exorcisms and healings. When he sent out seventy two followers to preach and heal he specifically warned them: 'However, do not rejoice that the spirits submit to you but rejoice that your names are written in heaven' (Luke: v 20). What he lacked by being restricted to a first-century world view, he made up for with his profound understanding of human nature. The number of times that Jesus was accused of being possessed should act as a further warning to his followers about being too quick to diagnose demons.

Nevertheless the early church continued to exorcize demons. It often got a reputation for having the most effective exorcists around. Later the church incorporated its rites of exorcism into a formal liturgy. In much the same way that the spontaneous gifts of the Spirit petered out and Christian values and tradition took their place, so spontaneous exorcisms waned and occasional and formal rites largely superseded them. However, whenever religious bigotry or 'fundamentalism' was in the ascendant, religious authorities would use their powers of 'discernment' to see the devil in people and despatch them without ceremony. The Cathars persecuted by the Catholic Church, the heretics burned at the stake following the Reformation, and the witch hunts in Europe and puritan New England are evidence of this. The tradition of scapegoating, and labelling other beliefs as devilish, goes back to St Paul watching the stoning of Stephen (and beyond) and is in healthy enough condition today.

Before the Charismatic renewal, exorcism and demon possession was more familiar terrain for the Gothic novelist than the average priest. Paradoxically, the advent of the modern exorcist has largely been a return to medievalism. In the UK the resurgence of exorcism or deliverance (as it is generally known) has been, at the very least, a mixed blessing. Whatever merits its practitioners may claim for it, in the last 25 years it also appears to have led to bigotry, mental illness, sexual abuse and death. It has proved to be a highly dangerous practice, particularly among those most likely to find themselves on the exorcist's couch, that is the mentally or emotionally unstable.

By the mid-1960s concern about exorcism arose in the Church of England. The Rt Revd Robert Mortimer, then Bishop of Exeter, decided to bring together priests, theologians and psychiatrists to form a commission looking into exorcism. He was anxious because the church lacked knowledge or experience, while an increasing number of people seemed to be approaching the church for help in this area. In 1972 the commission published a report, *Exorcism*, which was a discussion document, offering guidelines for those working in the area. The first point of the report stated: 'It cannot be overstressed that, as it is usually understood, the concept of demonic possession is extremely dubious.' The points made in the report emphasize that all medical (physical and psychological) avenues should be explored before carrying out an exorcism. It adds that an absence of medical problems should not be taken to prove that a person is possessed: 'the diagnosis of demonic possession must rest on precise and positive criteria.' The report stresses that for those apparently in need of exorcism, training in the normal Christian life, and belonging to and practising their faith in a Christian community, may well render exorcism redundant. If exorcism proves necessary, then it should be carried out by a priest experienced in the area, acting under the bishop's authority, usually with a licence to exorcize. It insists that a local parish priest should not take it upon himself to carry out exorcisms: 'It is not a field which forms a part of the ordinary duties of the pastoral ministry for which a parish priest may properly be considered to be competent.'

Two years after the publication of the Bishop of Exeter's report, an attempted exorcism involving an Anglican clergyman led to a brutal and bloody murder. Although there have been other deaths linked with exorcism in the UK, the notorious 'Barnsley case' is probably the most horrifying and is certainly responsible for catalyzing public debate about exorcism. The case centred on Michael and Catherine Taylor, a couple with five children, living in Ossett, near Barnsley. They were recent converts and in September 1974 agreed to a local Christian fellowship holding a meeting in their house. At their first meeting, choruses were sung and a young woman called Marie administered communion at the end of the meeting. Days later the Taylors hosted another meeting, and Marie started shaking uncontrollably and speaking in tongues. Afterwards she led an impromptu exorcism on one of those present. Michael Taylor then began to speak in tongues and to shake involuntarily to the extent that he was holding onto furniture and knocking it down. Three days later he believed that he had seen the devil who had told him to kill himself. He told members of the fellowship, and later in the day, when Marie visited, he kissed her on the lips.

The next fellowship meeting was held in Barnsley with a local vicar present. Michael told the group that he had been seduced, and it was decided that he should confess to God and that those present should pray over him. The following morning Michael told his wife to remove all religious books and artifacts from the house. That night, he said that he was frightened of the silence and he played the radio until sunrise. The next day, the Taylor family were being taken for a drive by a member of the fellowship, when Michael let out a terrifying scream, frightening the five children. They decided that a visit to the vicar who had been present at Michael's confession might be appropriate. On arrival at St Thomas' vicarage, Mr Taylor's behaviour had deteriorated. He was violent and unruly, hitting the vicar, throwing the cat through a window and food onto the floor. The Taylors' children were taken upstairs and put to bed, and it was agreed that Mr Taylor was in need of exorcism. A local Methodist minister and his wife who described themselves as 'practitioners in exorcism' were contacted, as well as a local Methodist preacher from Barnsley.

An all night exorcism was planned, with six exorcists present (both ministers and their wives, the local preacher and a member of the fellowship group), and at twelve o'clock the exorcism commenced in the vestry at the side of the church. The exorcists, however, were divided in their diagnoses. The Methodist minister said that God had told him that Mr Taylor needed psychiatric help. The vicar's wife was convinced that Mr Taylor had been 'pledged' to Satan and that Satan had used the 'power' of the moon to give Mr Taylor the desire to murder. The Revd Vincent decided to continue with the exorcism although there were no people with medical expertise present. Mr Taylor was laid face upwards on a pile of hassocks, and the exorcists took it in turns to pray over him and to order demonic spirits to leave him. They placed a crucifix in his mouth and Mr Taylor's own wooden cross was burned. He confessed to a variety of sins including lewdness, heresy, blasphemy and masochism. They told him that he had also committed incest and bestiality, sins which Mr Taylor later said he had no knowledge of. At times during the exorcism Mr Taylor went into spasms, writhing maniacally on the ground, puffing, panting and screaming.

By sunrise the exorcists believed that they had rid Mr Taylor of over forty demons. The vicar's wife was convinced that there were recalcitrant demons of violence, murder and insanity, that had refused to budge. They decided to deal with them at a later date and drove Mr Taylor and his wife home. The children were taken to stay with the grandparents. At 9.30 the following morning Mrs Taylor shouted to a visiting neighbour to go away because she believed herself to be possessed by an evil presence. Within thirty minutes she was dead. Mr Taylor had torn out her eyes, gouged out her face and left her dying, choking on her own blood. He was later found naked and bloody, aimlessly walking along a road. He was committed to Broadmoor, the special secure hospital.

According to Bishop Dominic Walker, the Church of England's chief adviser on healing and deliverance, twenty years later, the situation is getting worse. Walker reports an increase in the number of clients who are damaged by maverick Charismatic exorcists. Despite the guidelines in the Church of England, so-called 'rogue priests' carry out exorcisms without reference to their bishop. However, because the vicars currently have 'freehold' responsibility to act according to their conscience before God within their parish, the church is relatively powerless to act. Moreover, most people seeking Walker's advice come from Christian fellowships or non-denominational networks. The experiences of his clients are completely unregulated and bear no resemblance to the traditional rite of exorcism.

Although Walker is licensed to exorcize he says that he carries out less than one exorcism per year. Most of his time is spent undoing the damage that maverick exorcists have done. He says: 'I deal with an increasing number of counsellees who are suffering severe emotional problems following involvement with so-called exorcists on the fringe of the Charismatic movement.' Some have been told that they are possessed by demons of nicotine, alcohol, abortion, lust, promiscuity, homosexuality and bed wetting. 'People have come to me who are suicidal, believing that they are beyond God's help', he adds.

Despite Bishop Walker's circumspect approach to exorcism (which reflects the Church of England's official guidelines), there are others within the Anglican church who have a much more extreme view. Graham Dow, the Bishop of Willesden, has similar views to many of the self-styled exorcists. He has appeared several times on the platform of the fundamentalist Charismatic group 'Ellel Ministries', considered by many to be one of the most extreme organizations working in the area. Bishop David Pytches, who leads the thriving Anglican Charismatic church, St Andrew's, Chorleywood, has also publicly endorsed the work of the London Healing Mission, a healing centre that has sexually abused and severely damaged several people.

Bishop Graham Dow makes his views clear in *Deliverance*, a booklet published by Sovereign World Publishers. Following a foreword by Simon Barrington-Ward, Bishop of Coventry, Dow starts modestly enough, stressing that he sees deliverance (exorcism) as an unspectacular ministry which should take place 'alongside prayer for healing, confession, counselling, medical and psychiatric help, each form of knowledge making its own contribution to the healing process.' He points out that in most developing countries the assumption is that there are demonic spirits and that we should be open to this as a possibility. Dow also states that he believes that the presence of evil spirits in Britain is widespread. In a chapter entitled 'Clues to recognizing the Presence of Evil Spirits' which he offers 'cautiously, but on the basis of several years' experience of the ministry of deliverance', Dow outlines 29 pointers to demonic 'infestation'. One of his 'clues' is a person's countenance. Dow says: 'On several occasions I have seen the presence of a spirit in a person's face, looking at their countenance with my natural sight. This needs great care lest a normal fear or similar emotion be attributed to a spirit. It is possible, however, to see evil in a person's eyes; a false or artificial smile can be another indication.' While door to door salesmen would do well to avoid darkening Dow's door, he fails to explain exactly how (or by what criteria) one exercises 'great care' in discerning the bona fide demon.

Dow says that traumatic events such as traffic accidents, sexual abuse, bereavement, war or becoming a refugee may lead to demonic possession. He explains: 'The emotions of shock and pain go very deep and make the human spirit very vulnerable to an evil spirit coming to reinforce the pattern of brokenness. The ground of entry for the spirit is the fear, or similar emotion, which is a falling short of God's perfection and therefore sin, in the fullest sense of the word.' Dow earlier relates an incident in which he 'picked up' a spirit of fear of dying of cancer. He also believes that one can inherit spirits from traumas that have historically affected one's ancestors, and says that he has found deliverance to be needed for some whose ancestors have been involved in mining, a traumatic profession.

Being an unwanted child, and experiencing rejection from the womb to the children's home, is another possible entry route for demons. A sense of the presence of dead relatives, Dow suggests, 'may be an evil spirit which was attached to the dead person and is now seeking to transfer its power'. Celebrating communion with a family tree on the altar is a suggested possible source of relief from troubles with spirits of dead relatives. Even one's dress sense, car colour and house furnishing may indicate a demonic presence. One of Dow's clues is 'repeated choice of black for dress or car; markedly unrestful colour schemes for dress or house decor'. Addictions including drugs, alcohol, gambling, and eating disorders may be indications. Dow writes: 'Anorexia, I believe, usually involves a destructive spirit.' With similar pastoral sensitivity, Dow blithely states: 'In the case of abortion, spirits of rejection, murder and death are likely.' Naturally enough, the 'unnatural sexual acts' are mentioned as another possible demonic indicator.

In the chapter entitled 'Driving out the Evil Spirits', Dow makes clear his belief that demons can travel down the generational line. He believes that one can inherit the sins and demons of one's ancestors. He says: 'More difficult to shift are the spirits passed down relating to sins from several generations back. A complex weave of sins can be built up over several generations and there can be a multiple spirit presence.' It can be so confusing that it is 'sometimes essential to receive knowledge direct from God about the sin at the point of entry'. In the same chapter Dow explains that coughing and vomiting can be signs of demons leaving the person. He points out: 'Most spirits leave through the mouth; some leave in the way they came, for example, through the eyes, the sexual orifices, or the fingers.'

Dow appears to oppose the Anglican guidelines when he suggests that it is impractical alway Dow stresses that one should carry out the ministry of exorcism 'under authority' of one's church, he also appears to suggest that training is not necessary since Jesus carried out exorcisms 'by command'. He bemoans the Church of England's current position, saying: 'One of the problems of the Church of England is that it is not yet accepted that prayer for deliverance is routine prayer. The presence of evil spirits is treated as a rare phenomenon requiring great caution. In many dioceses no deliverance ministry is to be attempted without reference to the bishop or whoever he designates. This is impractical if spirits are widespread and mostly not very powerful (such as those I picked up).'

Dow's approach may seem like a potentially dangerous charter, yet, strangely, for someone with a pastoral ministry, the damage that such practices could do does not appear to be his main priority. He says in his chapter on recognizing clues of the demonic: 'I am prepared to risk making mistakes in order to open up possibilities that may not have been thought of, and which, when tried, lead to effective ministry.' It is not clear whether he is prepared to recognize that mistakes may be deeply damaging.

Deliver Us From Evil

Lynn's story started when she first became a Christian. She was living in London, working as an administration manager for a life insurance company. A colleague invited her to All Souls Langham Place, where she heard the Revd John Stott, a well respected Anglican preacher. She bought his book and became a Christian after reading it. Meanwhile Julie, Lynn's daughter, became a Christian independently, through her manager at work in Nottingham. Her marriage was going through a difficult time, she was lonely and Julie got involved in a local church. In 1989, after trying to work at the marriage, feeling emotionally distressed, she left her husband and went to live with Lynn. They believed that God was telling them to move to Mansfield, where they joined a Baptist church.

One morning when Julie was at church she started coughing. At the end of the service, an ex-missionary called Jane told Julie that she had been coughing because a demon was trying to leave her body. As a naïve and earnest young Christian, Julie believed her and agreed to be exorcized by Jane and her husband, Kenneth, who was a church elder. Later in the week she went to see them, and they quizzed her about her sex life, private habits, anything that could cause a blockage with God. Kenneth told her that he believed that Julie might be possessed because demons had come into her from her mother when she was in the womb. 'I was horrified to think that I was possessed of the devil because of something that my mother had done', Julie says. 'I saw pictures of black snakes writhing around inside me.'

Julie went through five weeks of exorcism with Kenneth and two other women from the church. During this time she was 'exorcized' of scores of demons, on one occasion an exorcism lasted five hours. 'Each time I would be manifesting physical reactions like coughing or groaning, which they believed were the demons struggling inside me, trying to stay put. It was normal for me to be crying or screaming, to be writhing around on the ground out of control. All the time I was thinking, "God help me get through this," Julie explains. There were demons of fornication, sexual abuse, false gods. 'Kenneth was particularly interested in sexual sins. Once he said that God had told him that there was a demon connected with my breasts" ', Julie says.

Julie was continually told that she had to cut her 'soul ties' (emotional bonds that some exorcists believe spirits can travel along) with her mother, and that you have to pay for the sins of your ancestors. She was told not to wear make-up or hats because these could stop the demons from leaving her. Towards the end of the five weeks, Kenneth told Julie not to give her mother any of the money which she was due from the sale of her house. 'I felt that I couldn't trust my Mum, I felt that there was something evil in the family. They were suggesting that she was a witch', Julie says 'They pushed a wedge right between us, and I went to live alone as quickly as I could.'

Lynn was visiting her minister, Pastor Bell, at her Baptist Church. She went to confide in him and to ask his advice about her deteriorating relationship with Julie, her 28 year old daughter. Both of them were Christians, both members of the same church, but Lynn was disturbed because Julie was behaving strangely, was distant and suspicious. Pastor Bell kept asking about Lynn's childhood, and she was puzzled, but thought that it was what counsellors did. Midway through the conversation Pastor Bell stared deep into her eyes and said commandingly: 'Who are you?' He then started talking to the demons that he thought were inside her. Within minutes Lynn was dizzy, out of control, and the room went black. 'I started coughing, I fell to the floor, I started writhing about on the floor, I was crying and he proceeded to exorcize me', Lynn says. Together with his wife, Mary, he prayed over her, telling her that God wanted to rid her of the evil spirits. Although it was involuntary, it was the beginning of eighteen months of weekly exorcisms, which got more and more outlandish, including lurid stories of child sacrifice and Satanic sexual abuse, and which left Lynn psychotic, jobless, friendless and emotionally in tatters. It was also the beginning, Lynn now realizes, of a nervous breakdown.

Meanwhile, Lynn was still attending church without any idea of what the church elder, Kenneth, had been doing with Julie, but increasingly confused about her relationship with Julie, which had always been close. It was this that led to her fateful 'counselling session'-cum-exorcism with Pastor Bell. However, it was during the following eighteen months of counselling sessions/exorcisms that things got worse. 'I felt emotionally raped', says Lynn 'In those sessions I had to confess everything in my life that could be judged by another human being.' Often when she shared the 'sin', or the feeling, she was told that she was possessed by a demon of that sin, which was controlling her and cutting her off from God. Lynn was told that she had demons of nicotine, murder, fornication, sexual abuse – even a demon of nothing. During this period she stopped sleeping and started seeing pictures: 'Basically I couldn't sleep, I was terrified; I had a very fitful doze for an hour or so once morning approached', she explains.

The pictures originated with Pastor Bell. He told her that God had shown him a vision of Lynn on an inverted cross covered in snakes. He asked whether she had been involved with witchcraft; he was convinced that she had. It was at this highly suggestive point that Lynn started seeing her own pictures, which she interpreted as childhood memories. Lynn's first picture was of being tied onto an inverted cross and held over a snake pit by a doctor at his surgery. 'The pictures came out during the eighteen months of exorcism, and formed a story of events that I thought had happened between the ages of four and seven,' Lynn explains. Lynn believed that her real father was a local doctor and a lay reader in St Mary's Church. She told Pastor Bell that he was a Satanist, and that her mother, who died when she was seven, was High Priestess in the coven which met in the crypt of St Mary's Church. 'I was born specifically for sacrificing myself to Satan. When I was four years old I went to his surgery and was sexually abused by him to be made ready for Satan', Lynn explains. She went on to tell stories of being a child prostitute for American airforce personnel who attended the Satanic meetings for sex and paid her with chocolate. The GIs produced babies for the coven, who were sacrificially killed in Satanic ceremonies before their bodies were burnt in the secret oven hidden in the crypt.

Another of Lynn's pictures was of being raped on a gravestone by the devil in the form of the jackal-headed Egyptian god, Anubis. She was then made to drink his semen. In another picture Lynn believed that she had a twin sister who was sacrificed at birth and who had really been called Lynn. Lynn believed that this imaginary twin had taken her name with her to the grave, and she told Pastor Bell that her real name was Elizabeth. She then received a letter from Pastor Bell, addressing her as Elizabeth. 'Pastor Bell believed every word and so did I. He seemed eager to believe the pictures, he did not think to ask questions or check things out, and I was in no fit state to do so', Lynn explains.

Having been exorcized of literally hundreds of demons, Lynn was psychotic. On one occasion after a morning service, she had been thrust into a room and forcibly held on the ground and exorcized by several members of the church. 'I was in tatters, I was a complete emotional wreck, I couldn't even go out shopping without getting distraught and confused', she recalls. The final straw came when the pastor's wife chastised her for being self-obsessed. She told Lynn to pull herself together and to count her blessings. At this point Lynn 'phoned the pastor and his wife up to break contact with them. 'They didn't give a damn,' Lynn recalls: 'They'd made me completely dependent on them, but the more I saw them the worse I got.' Weeks later they came to call on Lynn. 'They asked how I was, and I told them I was awful but that I did not want to speak to them', she says. She asked them to leave but they refused, saying that they could not leave her in such a state. 'They only left when I started screaming at them, begging them to leave', she adds.

Soon after, Julie and Lynn became close again, largely because Julie was trying to help her Mum to cope. One Sunday they drove up to Ellel Grange in Lancashire, the centre run by Ellel Ministries, a group who specialize in demonology and exorcism. They arrived hoping that Ellel's director, Peter Horrobin, the UK's best known teacher on exorcism, could help. He was not there and they were reluctantly allowed in for a cup of coffee and a quick prayer. 'That was our last hope and they rejected us; they only let us in grudgingly, and then gave us about half an hour of their time', Lynn says.

It was only when her doctor referred her to a psychiatrist that Lynn began to put her life back together. She was given drugs to control her feelings, and the pictures which had kept her awake for years began to subside. She realized that the pictures came from her pastor's suggestions and her own imagination. She visited St Mary's Church and discovered that it did not have a crypt. Then one morning Lynn woke up and said to herself 'Demons don't exist.' She returned to the Bells' and told them with what she describes as a calm fury, that what they were doing was dangerous. They listened quietly but did not offer an apology. Nearly three years on, Lynn and Julie have thrown their Bibles in the bin and describe themselves as atheists. 'If there is a God', Lynn says 'then when I die I shall have words with him.' Her psychiatrist pronounced Lynn well after nearly two years of consultations, although she still feels emotionally damaged by her experiences and is perpetually tired.

Pastor Bell was unwilling to comment on his relationship with Lynn or whether weekly exorcisms occurred during her time in his church, although he agreed that she had attended the church. However, when asked about Lynn's rejection of the stories that came from her pictures, he says 'That's okay, if that's where she's got to.' Concerning his judgments about whether or not people are possessed, he says: 'I would be seeking God about it', adding, 'I would be very, very careful about getting into that realm but I'd be open.' He stressed that he would only get into the area of exorcism and deliverance with the person's consent, but he would consult with members of his church rather than the Baptist Union. He also 'tests' his prophesies and visions by asking other Christians about them and checking to see if they are consistent with the Bible. Though Pastor Bell conceded that he had received no training in exorcism, he said that his wife had attended Ellel Grange with another member of his congregation.

Ellel Ministries are, in one respect, a remarkable success story in terms of growth. They started in 1986, with a prayer support group who believed that God had told them to purchase Ellel Grange, a large country mansion just outside Lancaster. Led by Oxford educated Peter Horrobin, who had previously been running Christian bookshops, they believed that God had called them to buy the property and to set up a ministry of healing and counselling. As Ellel's publicity states:

> The purchase of Ellel Grange was in itself a miracle. The vision was shared with individual Christians and local churches and hundreds of gifts poured in. On the day of completion, when all the different

resources were put together, there was £6 too much in just over half a million pounds! This confirmed to us all that the Lord had brought the ministry into being and that He had laid it on the hearts of His people to give.

However, it was only after Ellel Grange was established as a ministry centre that the leaders believed that God was leading them towards a much greater emphasis on exorcism. As Horrobin relates in his book *Healing Through Deliverance*: 'When Ellel Grange was acquired in 1986, none of the pioneering team could have anticipated the pilgrimage that was to follow . . . No-one expected that deliverance ministry would be such a strategic part of healing.' Horrobin believes that he was guided by God to concentrate on exorcism and to awaken the church to it as a neglected part of the Christian life. Central to Ellel's ministry is their desire to teach Christians to carry out exorcisms. Ten years ago this would have been too specialized a 'ministry' to set up an organization for, but what Ellel are offering is clearly in step with the times, as is shown by their dramatic expansion.

By 1991 Ellel were running courses throughout the year at their seventy-bed centre near Lancaster, and it was becoming apparent that demand was outstripping supply. It was decided to open a centre in the south of England. Later that year they bought Glyndley Manor and grounds, partly with the substantial gifts of Christians who identified with Ellel's vision. By 1993 Ellel established Singing Waters, a base in Canada.

Next came their involvement in eastern Europe. In October, Ellel described their contacts in eastern Europe to several thousand delegates at their conference The Church Ablaze in Brighton. They planned to purchase land to build a training centre named Ur Retje in Hungary. By the end of the conference delegates had donated or pledged £178,000 to the project. Ellel Ministries believe that they were led by God to set up the centre to teach Christians in needy and 'spiritually poor' former communist countries. They held conferences in Budapest, Wroclaw, Poland and in St Petersburg, where Horrobin sought to deliver people from what he saw as the bondage of communism and oppression. In a fundraising letter Horrobin asked UK supporters for a 'sacrificial donation', raising the spectre of wealthy 'false religions' using the vacuum left by communism to spread their anti-Christian teachings. He wrote: 'There is a huge vacuum in the east, into which devotees of false religions (such as Buddhists, the New Agers, the Mormons and the JWs) are pouring vast amounts of resources. They are starting to capture the minds of a generation. Can we stand by complacently and watch the enemy make such enormous inroads? Here is one way in which we can do something to establish a Christian bridge-head into eastern Europe.' He concludes: 'Please do not dismiss this brochure as "just another appeal". It is a unique opportunity to impact a vast and needy region. Please consider prayerfully what response you might make.' The cost of purchasing the land and building the centre was over two million pounds. The land has been purchased and building has begun.

Despite these pressing needs in eastern Europe, Ellel managed to find enough money to buy a third centre in the UK. In February 1994 Ellel bought the 35 acre Pierrepont Estate near Farnham, Surrey, for £2.15 million. The former Catholic private school, with student accommodation, a teaching block and a large conference hall, was to become an international training centre in exorcism and healing. Once again Ellel made huge efforts to raise enough money to secure the deposit on the estate. They had approximately three weeks in which to reach the £322,500 for the deposit, and once again they called on the spectre of the 'false religions' bogeyman to encourage supporters to donate.

In a letter to supporters in the local area they claimed that if they did not receive the necessary funds, then the Unification Church or Moonies were set to buy the house. The letter suggested that they were a mainstream Christian organization working with victims of drug abuse, sexual abuse and abortion as well as providing 'help for disabled people'. The letter did not include Ellel's belief that abortion, sexual abuse and drug taking would lead to possession which should be dealt with by exorcism. Against this benign, gentle Christian image was set the spectre of the Moonies. The letter stated that while making their offer:

> they became aware of fierce competition from the Unification Church (the 'Moonies') from the USA,

which organization is trying to make a major inroad into Europe through a UK headquarters. Perhaps the nature of the Unification Church and the 'mind control' methods it uses in its work, especially among young people, may not be known to you, but the spiritual implications for this area and for the whole of southern England, are very serious indeed.

Unfortunately, Ellel did not check the veracity of the rumour (indeed, when asked, they were unsure where it had originated). George Robertson, the Unification Church's UK spokesman, said that they had never heard of Pierrepont Estate, let alone put in a bid to buy it; they already had a UK base. He went on to suggest that their 'bad name' had been used as a means of raising funds. He informed their lawyer and said, 'Perhaps we should consider leasing out our name to Christian groups in need of raising money quickly.' Ellel's Pierrepont administrator, Jill Southern, admitted that they had made a mistake, but claimed that the fundraising letter was written in good faith. The purchase went ahead, and in 1996 they started teaching students from around the world to carry out exorcisms.

Such is the rise and rise of the UK's (possibly the world's) biggest exorcists' organization. But what are their doctrines, what is the message that they appear to be having such success in spreading? In essence Ellel believe that all areas of life can be invaded by evil spirits and that exorcism (or deliverance, as they prefer to call it) is a key part of Christian ministry, vastly underused by the church. The Revd Peter Andrews (a vicar in the Willesden area of London, whose bishop is Graham Dow) who has spent time researching Ellel, believes that the writings of Peter Horrobin, Ellel's leader, are almost pornographic in their obsession with sex. In a circular to clergy within his area, he points out that exorcists with this approach, 'by rediscovering primitive superstition and primeval fears are set to grip those trapped in their grasp, in a world of continuing terror and darkness.' He says: 'The particularly frightening aspect of deliverance ministries is that, although Horrobin acknowledges that there are other forms of healing, there are very few people who are not included in his description of highly likely candidates for possession.'

Horrobin appears to have a knack for finding 'demons' in people's vulnerable areas, and a particular inclination for discerning demons related to people's sexuality. In his second book on exorcism, *Healing Through Deliverance 2*, Horrobin writes: 'There are few people I counsel who do not have some sort of sexual skeleton in the cupboard.' He adds:

> In recent years I have ministered to many elderly Christians, some of them with well-known and established ministries. In the confidence of the counselling room they have shared their inner problems, and some have been broken hearted over the way they have continuous struggles with temptations, often of a sexual nature, that they have been powerless to fight off. In many cases, such people have never understood that they are not just fighting temptation from without, or their fallen flesh nature, but are struggling with demons within which have never been recognized.

Horrobin also believes that demons have particular entry points into people. These entry points (by which he means routes) do sometimes relate to bodily orifices, but may be emotional feelings, experiences or interests, as well as illness. One can also inherit demons, according to Horrobin, as a sort of diabolical heirloom. Indeed in the notes for Ellel's Deliverance Ministry Training Course, twenty-eight demonic entry points are noted, but listening to Horrobin speak it is clear that there is virtually nothing that cannot lead to picking up a demon. Sometimes demons have to exit via the same place that they entered. One vicar relates going on an early Ellel course in which he was told that sometimes it was necessary to pour Ribena (substitute communion wine) onto people's genitals to cleanse them of demons related to sexual sin which had entered there. Another unfortunate young man claims he had Ribena poured down his trousers after asking Horrobin if he could go out with his daughter. He was accused of having a demon of lust and was subjected to an impromptu and rather sticky exorcism.

Unlikely though Horrobin's ideas may seem, to vulnerable people seeking help in a paranoid universe, such ideas are often seen as the natural outworking of living in a spiritual warzone. In October 1993 3000 people listened unquestioningly to his homespun demonology. In a seminar called *Specialist Aspects of Deliverance* Horrobin described the mechanics of gay and lesbian sex in lurid detail and then explained that 'demons' of homosexuality could be caused by parents committing unnatural sex. But 'gay demons' could also be allowed into the children while washing one's children in the bath; any touching that was to cleanse was good and godly, but if one's feelings altered momentarily then the possibility of a spirit of 'perverted sex', or homosexuality, arose. In the same eclectic seminar, Horrobin explained that accident black spots were in fact demons at work. With echoes of Frank Peretti, he said: 'Spirits of curse are given rights over a stretch of road to cause death.'

If the audience were feeling traumatized by such information, they were not about to be relieved. Traumas, they were told, can allow demons to enter. 'It may only be for a fraction of a second, we are so vulnerable and wide open that the Enemy can come and bring a spirit into us through fear, through trauma.' Horrobin told a story of a nurse who slipped and put her back out of joint and nearly dropped a dying patient while helping to move her. During that moment of pain a demon left the dying lady and entered the nurse. As he explained, 'When people die, demons do not; they just look for a new house.' This entry route for demons attached to dead people is called transference, and Horrobin believes that Christians working in the medical profession need to take especial care. Undertakers too, one assumes.

In a seminar called simply *Deliverance Ministry* Horrobin develops his views. He describes the experience of 'déjà vu' and explains reassuringly that the impossibility of our having been somewhere before makes sense: 'It's probably that the demons have been there before.' Any form of obsession can lead to possession. When pet owners become too fond of their pets, they open themselves up to the spirit of the animal. That is why, he argues, people so often start to resemble their pets. Demons of chocolate, coffee, tea, alcohol and nicotine may also need delivering, if they assume too much importance in people's lives. Horrobin tells a tale of exorcising a man from a demon of peppermints, which before the exorcism had made him a slave to his addiction.

Although one assumes that these nutritional demons do not go too deep, there are much more worrying aspects of Horrobin's beliefs. He claims not to have come across a psychiatric condition that has not involved demons. In his *Deliverance Ministry* seminar, he stated: 'I haven't yet ministered to anyone who was seriously sexually abused who did not also need deliverance.' He added: 'Approximately one in two women who come to Ellel Grange for help have been sexually abused.' In the same seminar, he referred to carrying out exorcisms on two and three year olds. He also said: 'After some of the heavier ministries that we've done from time to time, I've seen people who were physically bleeding after the demons had come out.'

These may be examples of extreme and disturbing practices, but what may be equally worrying is Horrobin's story of a 'spirit of disagreement' in a church council meeting. Horrobin relates: 'When opposition mounted, he (the man disagreeing) started speaking out the things that the demon wanted him to say.' If it is possible to be labelled as a demoniac just for disagreeing with Horrobin, one wonders how his clients cope when they consider his diagnosis inappropriate or ill-judged. Might they not be tempted to go along with it?

Despite their extreme beliefs, Ellel's counselling course is certificated by the Association of Christian Counsellors, Ellel Ministries are a member of the Evangelical Alliance, and they are attracting mainstream and high profile evangelical speakers to their conferences. It may not be a surprise that Bishop Graham Dow has appeared on their platforms, but the presence of Jackie Pullinger (who for many was a sort of Protestant Mother Teresa, ministering to heroin addicts in Hong Kong) when she spoke at Ellel's Into All the World conference in Blackpool in 1995 was a sign of their increasing influence. It is probably a conservative estimate to say that over ten thousand Christians are exposed to their teaching annually. Their meteoric growth could be both a symptom and a cause of a sinister and harsh form of superstition which is sweeping over the Charismatic church.

NB. All the names in Lynn and Julie's story have been changed.

The Notting Hill Sexorcist

Like many of the members of the congregation at the London Healing Mission, Mary was middle-aged, smartly turned out and female. The mission was well known as a quiet, Anglican-based centre of healing and fellowship. The well worn dowdiness of the cosy basement 'chapel' was reassuring in itself. In the midst of frenetic, neon-lit Notting Hill, the London Healing Mission was a comforting reminder of 'how it used to be'. To the scores that arrived for the low key Charismatic communion and healing services, it was a shelter from the storm. And despite the preponderance of middle-aged women with plummy accents, it was a shelter that clearly had a wide appeal. It was not unusual to see Laura Ashley dresses mingling with the hip street clothes of young blacks or the rough, ill-fitting hand knits of reformed alcoholics and beggars. What is more remarkable is that at the London Healing Mission members of such diverse groups had time for each other.

It was not only the 1950s' ambience that was so comforting about this tiny centre in the middle of West London. It was also the proprietors, who resonated decency, reassurance and an 'old world' set of values. The tall, greying, bespectacled Revd Andy Arbuthnot, who headed the mission, was the epitome of upper class respectability. He was educated at Eton, then served as a Captain in the Scots Guards, before taking over the directorship of his family's banking business. During his time working in the City he was also a director of the Sun Alliance insurance company, and chairman and chief executive of another old family company, Arbuthnot Latham Holdings. He had also found time to contest the Houghton-le-Spring constituency as a Conservative candidate in 1959. After retiring from the City, Arbuthnot was ordained as an Anglican priest in 1975, to work in the non-stipendiary ministry.

Arbuthnot's wife, Audrey, was from a similarly well heeled background. With her lightly powdered face, tightly bobbed mouse hair and her conservative dress sense, Audrey bore a striking resemblance to the Queen. A more upstanding couple would be hard to imagine, and during their fifteen or so years at the mission, people responded in ever increasing numbers. Perhaps the poorer people who attended the mission found their gentle, respectful class manners appealing – a glimpse of old fashioned decency and certainty; perhaps the wealthier members of the congregation (many of whom joined the healing team) liked the understated, quietly Charismatic ways of the Arbuthnots. At any rate, hundreds felt that the Arbuthnots were to be trusted; they were a safe pair of hands. As their ministry expanded they were invited to national Christian platforms to speak about their experiences in the healing ministry. They were well known and respected in that slightly cloying, unquestioning and conformist environment, the Charismatic Christian ghetto.

When Mary first arrived with a friend, she had heard that it was a small, peaceful Charismatic centre which ran a couple of friendly weekly services. At the time she was working as a catalogue model and beautician, and bringing up her three daughters (from two previous marriages) alone. Money was tight, but generally she made ends meet, enjoyed work and had positive relationships with her daughters. She was impressed enough with her visit to start attending the weekly Thursday evening communion and healing services. It was at these services that Arbuthnot started inviting Mary to special counselling and prayer sessions. She had confided in him about her eldest daughter, who was missing, and Arbuthnot suggested that they met to pray about it. They did, and Mary found sharing her worries comforting and helpful.

Mary rarely made appointments, but during the week Mr Arbuthnot would 'phone to say that someone else had cancelled an appointment and would offer her the time instead. During the counselling and prayer sessions, Arbuthnot started to ask Mary about her childhood. She told him that her memories of childhood were blank because she had been sexually abused and wanted to forget about it. Arbuthnot insisted that God could not want her wilfully to ignore part of her past; God, he said, would seek to heal the memories, to redeem the past. As they talked about Mary's experiences of sexual abuse, Arbuthnot suggested that they use 'pet names' for bodily parts. Romeo and Juliet were the names for Mary's breasts, Flossie was her genitals and Oscar was the abuser's penis.

At this time of counselling, Mary's friends noted that she was losing confidence and becoming increasingly neurotic. Belinda Belousa, a friend of many years' standing, says: 'Mary was naturally confident and fiercely independent, but during this stage she was becoming unstable, she was losing self-belief.' Mary confirms this and explains that she was convinced that the Arbuthnots were the answer to her problems. 'I did not know how to deal with my problems and they'd convinced me that my sexual abuse needed facing; it all seemed to make sense at the time', Mary recalls. Contrary to good counselling practice, the Arbuthnots became substitute parents to Mary as she regressed into a childhood state for large parts of the day. The Arbuthnots bought her cuddly toys, and Mary would sit on the floor playing with them as Mr and Mrs Arbuthnot prayed over her.

Mary says that during one session she was confronted by Arbuthnot standing directly in front of her, sprinkling her with holy water. She asked him to stand back, explaining that his closeness was unnerving her. He ignored her and continued sprinkling her with water, and after more pleas with him, she lost her temper, knocked the water to the ground and headed for the door. Arbuthnot blocked the door, convinced that Mary's outburst was demonic, and called his wife to come up. 'Whatever I said to explain myself, they interpreted as a demon speaking through me. It was terrifying. They were convinced that it was a demon that had knocked the water to the floor, but it was me. I was really angry', Mary says. When Mrs Arbuthnot arrived, they continued sprinkling water on Mary and told her that she had a spirit of anti-Christ. She ended up on the floor, sobbing tears of fear and frustration.

Mary started to have nightmares, and despite her increasing dependence on the mission, she resolved several times not to return. On several occasions Mr Arbuthnot or his wife 'phoned and persuaded her to return for ministry. By this time Mary was finding working increasingly difficult; despite her beautician's training, she could not cover the dark shadows under her eyes and she felt unable to model clothes. Arbuthnot had asked her to give up modelling anyway; he felt it was 'unholy'.

At one of these sessions Mrs Arbuthnot told Mary that her parents had been Satanists, and she had been involved in Satanic rituals as a child and had been married to Satan. From this point on, each prayer and counselling meeting was an exorcism. Mary says: 'I believed that I was possessed by hordes of evil spirits. But if I ever disagreed with what they were saying, they said that it was a demon talking through me.' She would end up on the floor, sobbing, and vomiting up what she believed were demons. Mary became increasingly traumatized, particularly because the sessions were physically painful. She was regularly pinned to the ground and was so badly bruised that she had to wear long sleeved shirts. 'The violence was incredible, they are both strong people, the horrors of what happened can't go down on paper', Mary says. She was told that she had demons of masochism, oral sex and death, as well as demons named after obscure Old Testament figures. The Arbuthnots took the concept of 'entry points' and 'exit points' seriously, interpreting Mary's coughs, sneezes or even yawns as demons leaving her. When Mary asked them why her condition was not improving after so much ministry, they told her that the demons were making her feel distressed as a way of discouraging her from returning.

After two years of ministry Mary was told that she had demons in her genitals. The Arbuthnots were convinced that Mary was possessed by a demon from her mother (called 'mummy') and that the only way to rid her of this demon was via 'internal ministries'. Mary says: 'I was called into the office and told that the spirit of mummy was really, really evil and the only way that they were going to get this demon out, along with all the childhood spirits that had gone in while I was being abused, was through internal ministry.' Mary was told that they would anoint her front and back passage with consecrated wine. 'I looked at Audrey', Mary remembers, 'and asked if she was sure that this was right, and she said that both she and Andy had prayed extensively about it and God had been very explicit about what they should do.' Mary was also told that five others were 'getting free' through internal ministry. She was also told that the concept of 'internal ministries' originated with a former Satanist who had told the Arbuthnots how effective Satanists found these rituals. Possibly the idea was that to fight the devil, they had to use his methods; certainly this ministry was coming to resemble the very things that it opposed.

Mary rejected the proposal but was told that without it she

would never be free of her mummy spirit. Exactly how the first session of internal ministries happened is unclear, but Mary is adamant that she did not give permission. She was invited to the mission for tea, and after discussing internal ministries with Mr Arbuthnot, she collapsed and later found the Arbuthnots taking her clothes off. Internal ministries took place regularly for over two years. Arbuthnot was ritualistic and superstitious in his approach, making the sign of the cross inside Mary with Dubonnet soaked fingers, in batches of seven. On other occasions he would make the sign of the cross on her breasts and buttocks before rubbing the Dubonnet in.

During this time, Arbuthnot became convinced that God had told him that his wife was to die and that he was then to marry Mary. He had been sending Mary secret romantic letters in which the roles of counsellor, priest, father and lover started to blur. In one letter dated February 18th, Arbuthnot mentioned internal ministry and Mary's fear of Mrs Arbuthnot doing it: 'Don't worry about demons in Romeo and Juliet. Remember I got several out last summer. Just tell Audrey that you can't bear her ministering to R and J, or inside you.' He signed the letter: 'Your friend, your brother, your lover and husband to be.' Other letters were signed: 'Papa, Andy, Lover and Husband to be.' It was almost as if Arbuthnot were deliberately pointing out the extent to which he was blurring roles.

Of the hundreds of letters that Arbuthnot sent, many are sexually explicit and full of romantic longing. According to Mary, she asked him not to write or 'phone on several occasions, and once confronted Audrey with her husband's infidelity. 'He just wouldn't take no for an answer and he knew that I needed both of them as substitute parents. I was dependent, but all the romantic stuff just frightened me', she says. Unfortunately for Mary, Arbuthnot began to blur the boundaries during his ministry sessions too. On occasions, having drunk a considerable amount of Dubonnet in communion rituals, Mary would end up naked and soaked in Dubonnet, which Arbuthnot believed would cleanse her of evil spirits. On several occasions when Mary 'came round from the spirit', she discovered Arbuthnot touching her. He told her that he was educating her sexually for their wedding day so that she would no longer be childlike.

Not surprisingly, Mary was confused to the point of becoming suicidal. The situation had developed into a mirror image of her childhood sexual abuse in which she expected love but received love and sex. She found it difficult to distinguish between Arbuthnot as her caring counsellor and her sexually frustrated husband to be. She tried to close her eyes to the seedy aspects of the letters, choosing to ignore them or interpret them as platonic. Yet she also believed that Arbuthnot's prophecy (or promise from God) must be true because he was such a strong 'godly' man, while at the same time realizing that it must be wrong for a husband to deceive his wife. Marriage to Arbuthnot (or anybody else) was not what Mary wanted; the idea terrified her. But if it was God's will, she told herself, she would go through with it.

At this stage Arbuthnot was paying money directly into Mary's account to help her financially. Initially, Mary had returned his cheques, but, she says, Arbuthnot found her account number and over a period of years paid over £22,000 to her. He told Mary to buy some clothes ready for him in case his frustrations got the better of him, and he were to leave Mrs Arbuthnot and come to live with Mary. On one occasion, Mary says, Mrs Arbuthnot confronted him with his infatuation and suggested that he talk to some Christian friend to sort it out. He refused because he was convinced of his 'promise', and he believed that his friends would tell him that it was sin. Arbuthnot appears to have deluded himself to the extent that he rationalized a completely hypocritical existence – one in which he would be publicly ministering at a Charismatic gathering called New Wine, at the same time as stealthily sending secret love letters to Mary. Justifying his behaviour as inspired by God, he was accountable to no-one and in a position to override anybody's objections to his behaviour.

Although Mary was dependent and childlike, she tried to confront Arbuthnot many times. Once, she had been lured to meet him (after a period of several months avoiding him) by being told that he was desperate to talk to her about something. Mary, not wanting him alone with her in her flat, suggested that they go for a walk on Putney Common. When they got there it became apparent that Arbuthnot was not in a desperate state; he simply wanted to see her. At the end of the meeting she was left on a railway station, bleeding badly from his unsolicited sexual attentions, and in tears. 'He did not seem to see what he had done to me, although I tried to tell him', Mary says. 'He was so convinced that he was right and that he was within God's will.'

Eventually, Mary and another victim of internal ministries approached the London Healing Mission trustees, Canon Sir Nicholas Rivett-Carnac and the Revd David Abel, to complain about internal ministries. Mary did not tell them about Arbuthnot's romantic letters and 'phone calls. They were told that while the trustees did not necessarily approve of the practice, they were unwilling to ban it. Mary then approached the late Bishop of Kensington, John Hughes, who interviewed Arbuthnot and then removed his license to officiate as an Anglican minister – effectively banning him from presiding at Anglican communion services. The Association of Christian Counsellors were Mary's next port of call. When Arbuthnot was confronted, he refused to accept that internal ministries were inappropriate as a form of ministry. He was expelled from the organization.

In 1994 Mary told the police, and they launched a major investigation into exorcism and internal ministries. Based in Notting Hill, the operation was called 'Operation Lentil' and involved a team of seventeen officers. Detective Inspector Turner, who led the operation, was shocked at the existence of such medieval practices and beliefs in the twentieth century. 'It was a bizarre land of Satanists and demons, a kind of fantasy world taken from a horror film. It took weeks to actually familiarize ourselves with the concepts and beliefs that people were living by', he says. Officers were sent up to Ellel Grange and to other centres practising exorcism. During their investigations they came across others who had received internal ministries at the hands of the Arbuthnots.

Mandy Pennys, one of these victims, agreed to join Mary in the police's criminal case against the Arbuthnots. Mandy was a former staff member who was sacked from the ministry team without explanation. When she asked about the sacking, the Arbuthnots agreed to take her back as long as she was willing to receive ministry. Mandy agreed and, like Mary before her, was told that she had been sexually abused by her parents in Satanic rituals. She too was offered Christian sexual rituals in the form of internal ministries, to rid her of the demons hiding in her genitals. She accepted and went through several Dubonnet-soaked marathon sessions, lasting up to ten hours at a time. Mandy told friends and broke free from the hold of the Arbuthnots.

After several months of investigation Detective Inspector Turner's team raided the London Healing Mission. They found the bottles of Dubonnet, the initialized tubs of Vaseline and the specially soundproofed room, just as Mary and Mandy had described. The Arbuthnots were subsequently charged with indecent assault, false imprisonment and actual bodily harm. Months later, against the wishes of Detective Inspector Turner, the Crown Prosecution Service dropped the charges. 'It was decided', he says 'that one of the problems evidentially was the issue of consent amongst those involved.'

Meanwhile, Arbuthnot had been busy rehabilitating himself in the Christian press. In a 'personal letter' in *Renewal* magazine, Arbuthnot said, 'My and Audrey's consciences are completely clear about every aspect of our ministry.' He continued: 'The support we have had from friends has been quite overwhelming: more than 150 letters expressing total disbelief in what the media have been saying, and giving us every encouragement.' The letter was cleverly worded, implying that internal ministries had not occurred. This was not the case; Arbuthnot had admitted in court that he had carried out internal ministries. He seemed set to continue his ministry, but it was an unfortunate coincidence that he referred to over 150 letters of support.

This was the exact number of love letters that Mary had secretly kept hidden. Arbuthnot must have been banking on the fact that Mary had destroyed them. It was only when she showed the letters to journalists, proving that Arbuthnot had been seeking to carry out a relationship with her (this had not been relevant to the police charges), that Arbuthnot had to face his actions and the London Healing Mission trustees had to act. I wrote a large feature for the *Observer*, exposing Arbuthnot's infatuation and his abusive practices, and days afterwards Arbuthnot and his wife retired from full time work at the mission (although it had been planned before). It was after this article appeared that Mr Arbuthnot was barred from ministering at the mission and internal ministries were banned. Yet strangely, Canon Sir Nicholas Rivett-Carnac, one of the mission's trustees, while acknowledging that internal ministries were damaging, claimed that one woman had benefited from it considerably.

The events at the London Healing Mission serve to illustrate several important points. First, they show clearly the dangers of practising a 'God said' style of ministry. To put oneself on a pedestal in this way has to be fraught with dangers. Arbuthnot is reported as saying to the police officers who arrested him: 'You can't judge me, God is my judge.' He clearly rode roughshod over any disagreement or questioning. He put his 'promise' to marry Mary above criticism and Christian morality and held to it with a doggedness which was probably fuelled by internal frustrations and problems. What is equally alarming is the way that Charismatic leaders attract unquestioning obedience and respect from followers and fellow leaders. Perhaps this blind faith reflects a desperate desire for certainty on the part of the followers: certainly it reflects shallowness and a curious morality. The idea of accepting that one's parents are sexually abusing Satanists because a plausible leader says so, would beggar belief in most circles. Not in desperate, gullible, and neurotic Charismatic ones. Such an uncritical concept of leadership is dangerous.

Second, in some ways it can be seen that the 'paranoid universe' that Arbuthnot and his wife seemed to inhabit bears a direct relation to Frank Peretti's dualistic vision. If everything is to be divided into good and evil in this way, then demons may indeed reside in any orifice that one's neuroses lead one to.

The final point is that the victims of maverick exorcists take on the exorcist's agenda. Both Mary and Mandy accepted, against their better judgement, that their parents had been Satanists. The idea had originated in the mind of the exorcist. Given the dualistic, superstitious and neurotic world view of many Charismatics involved in exorcism, is it really surprising that they project their lurid, sexually fixating agenda onto their victims? It is no surprise that they become like the thing that they hate; that their damaging rituals resemble the supposed rituals of their Satanic enemies. It is no surprise that they dehumanize and wound many of the people that they are seeking to help.

Toronto: The Feel God Factor

It was with glee that a congregation member at Holy Trinity Brompton explained how God moved in mysterious ways. 'Could there be a less likely place for God to start a major world-wide move than in a tiny church near Toronto Airport?' he asked. The apparent paradox of God choosing such an obscure unexceptional place for an 'outpouring' clearly appealed. 'It's a bit like the Son of God being born in a cattle shed', he added. 'God chooses the lowly, the places that make no sense according to human logic.'

Cattle sheds are not completely inappropriate. Holy Trinity Brompton is a thousand strong, well-to-do Anglican church in Knightsbridge, London, and my pre-Christmas visit there was a bit like a nativity scene. I was witnessing the Toronto Blessing, a phenomenon in which people fall down, laughing or crying or making uproarious animal noises. It originated in Canada and swept through the UK churches in the summer of 1994. After half an hour of Charismatic choruses and a short sermon, followed by more worship, people started simultaneously experiencing what looked like religious ecstasy and agony. They started collapsing, and it was then that I heard a loud mooing, then something that resembled a lion roaring. I moved to the front for a better view.

There was a young woman pogoing up and down, beaming. She looked at me as I disappeared from her consciousness, dissolving in what seemed like religious delirium tremens. To the left a young man rolled from side to side on the ground, groaning like a stuck pig. Yards away, behind the altar, was the young man on all fours roaring for all he was worth, arching his head backwards as his leonine roars grew louder and more confident. The girl opened her eyes and I asked her what was happening. She explained breathlessly, as she continued pogoing up and down, that she had been experiencing this for some weeks and that she did not know what was happening, but it was 'of God'. Later, the young man (whose 'manifestations' metamorphosed from groaning agony to convulsions of ecstatic laughter) told me that during these experiences

God was drawing him closer. His 'prayer life' was improved and he felt a greater desire to evangelize, to bring others to faith.

The Toronto Blessing had clearly swept through the church to dramatic effect. For weeks they had hundreds of people queuing down the street to attend their services. By October they had to put on an extra service to avoid turning people away. The church newspaper had a piece by church worker, Mrs Glenda Waddell, describing the effect of her recent visit to the Toronto Airport Vineyard church, the apparent source of this new outpouring. Before her pilgrimage, she had felt guilty and uneasy about her experience of uncontrolled laughing whenever 'the Holy Spirit was anywhere near'. She was strangely conscious of her thoughts and feelings while she was laughing (many seem to be aware of themselves during the phenomenon). She went to Toronto and her roaring and crying increased in volume. She attended a leaders' meeting and it was there that she believes God answered her questions about what she was experiencing. 'That room', she wrote, 'sounded like it was a cross between a jungle and a farm-yard. There were many, many lions roaring, there were bulls bellowing, there were donkeys, there was a cockerel near me, there were sorts of birdsong . . . everything you could possibly imagine. Every animal you could conceivably imagine you could hear.' She asked God what was going on and she believes that He told her that it was his way of stripping the church of its vanity. He told her that this had to happen before she could help 'win the world for Christ'. She returned to London without guilt or misgivings about the phenomenon, desperate for more of what she believed that the Holy Spirit was doing.

There are a number of theories about exactly where the Toronto Blessing originated, but it first became widely known at the Toronto Airport Vineyard church. There is a worldwide network of Vineyard churches led by John Wimber and subscribing to his 'signs and wonders' theology. In early 1994 the laughing, crying and grunting phenomenon started to occur each meeting, often going on for several hours. The Charismatic grapevine, notoriously sensitive to tremors of 'revival', spread the message, and soon Charismatic church leaders from around the world descended on Toronto in an unholy rush. Traditional holy places like Mecca and Lourdes have attracted millions for centuries, but approximately 500,000 pilgrims visited Toronto in two years, with no historical precedent. It is a phenomenal testament to the attraction of a 'divine' touch for Charismatic Christians.

However, this pilgrimage eschewed sackcloth and ashes (or other forms of spiritual discipline) in favour of jumbo jets, hire cars and hotels (offering special deals). Observers have noted that these pilgrims are predominantly white, middle class professionals. The concept that the Holy Spirit was somehow especially present in Toronto was unusual for Charismatics, who would traditionally dismiss pilgrimages and holy places as superstitious. Many pilgrims may be uneasy with this, yet most are clear that Toronto is the source of the blessing and that it is somehow 'diluted' when it is experienced in their churches at home.

The main route for the blessing into the UK was through the leaders of Holy Trinity Brompton and Bishop David Pytches, then priest of St Andrews, Chorleywood, and a number of 'New Church' leaders. The UK press (secular and Christian) reported the phenomenon, and soon Holy Trinity Brompton became a place of pilgrimage. Within a year it was estimated that as many as 3000 churches were experiencing the Toronto Blessing. Some were holding extra 'Receiving Meetings' to allow people to receive the blessing, several nights per week.

For many in the Charismatic movement the phenomenon was seen as the beginning of a national revival. Others were concerned at the unruly and apparently ludicrous phenomenon of animal noises, which they thought was probably hysterical and certainly contradicted Paul's teachings about church services being orderly. There was some concern that the blessing might split the Charismatic movement. A feature in the Evangelical Alliance's magazine in May 1995 stated: 'While no work of God takes place without a fleshly dimension, or even the possibility of demonic counterfeit, opinions differ markedly among evangelicals at present over precisely what is happening. Some have grave reservations . . . others speak of 1994 as a year of remarkable spiritual refreshing.' It concluded that time was needed to evaluate the phenomenon. Within months, leading Charismatic magazines like *Renewal* took a broadly positive line while emphasizing that what was important about the blessing was that it 'bore fruit', or more specifically, the 'fruits of the Spirit' (love, joy and peace) as recorded by the writer of the epistle to the Galatians.

Others even suggested that the Toronto blessing had, by circumventing the rational, broken down barriers between leaders and helped to unite the Charismatic church.

It was a shock when, in December 1995, John Wimber (whose ministry was seen as the obvious antecedent of the Toronto Blessing) expelled the Toronto Airport church from the Vineyard network. He said that the leaders of the Toronto church had repeatedly violated the guidelines and instructions that the Board of the Vineyard churches had given. Wimber stressed Vineyard churches were committed to a style of ministry that 'preserves the dignity of the individual' and said that they could not endorse or encourage 'exotic practices'. The Toronto church complained that they were offered no chance to appeal or discuss their expulsion. This split was played down by the Charismatic press and it had little effect on the prevalence of the 'blessing' in churches.

So what does the Toronto Blessing signify? Certainly this Charismatic phenomenon has generated few horror stories. Indeed it has brought more laughter than tears to observers and commentators. Dr Mark Stibbe, a priest and theologian based in Surrey, is broadly enthusiastic. After a visit to Toronto with his ministry at a low ebb, Dr Stibbe felt emotionally refreshed by his experiences. He endorses the teaching of the Toronto leadership, which explains the phenomenon as God's way of developing intimacy and preparing for the harvest of worldwide revival. He also believes that the phenomenon reflects a God who works within a culture and reveals Himself in ways that can be felt and understood by the society. Contemporary culture, he argues, is characterized by an increasing emphasis on the ecstatic, the subjective experiential, and the hedonistic, and thus the Holy Spirit has to make himself known through felt experiences rather than through reason or ethics alone. 'People need to experience God, and the Toronto Blessing is one way that this happens; it is then the churches' job to challenge the excesses of a purely subjective, experiential approach,' he says.

Graham Cray, principal of Ridley Hall theological college, is another apologist for the phenomenon, although he is concerned by the emphasis on Toronto as a geographical centre for the Holy Spirit. He has 'laughed in the Spirit' and claims that it has enhanced his capacity for empathy. 'It is not simply a feel-good experience which has led to spiritual navel-gazing; it has made me much more aware of suffering', he says. Cray believes that the Toronto Blessing offers white, rationalistic westerners the opportunity to integrate the physical and emotional aspects of spirituality with their more sober approach. Because it is sweeping through middle class congregations, Cray argues, it is bringing them closer to the experiences of traditionally working class Pentecostals, who have never had a problem expressing themselves physically. He suggests that it may be a symptom of so-called postmodern spirituality, because it is not based in the rational but in the experiential but he is concerned that among some there has been a tendency to drop their critical faculties. Although Cray believes that one possible cause for the 'blessing' is the deep sense of uncertainty and upheaval within society, which historically leads to an upsurge in supernatural phenomena, he stresses that this does not mean that it is not also an act of the Holy Spirit.

However, there are some who are concerned about the psychological motivations behind the manifestations. Dr Russell Blacker, a Christian psychiatrist, has observed the phenomenon on a number of occasions and believes that it can be explained psychologically. 'The Toronto experiences are very similar to ecstatic phenomena seen in other religions; they bear all the hallmarks of dissociation, and we do not need to invoke the Divine to explain them', he says. Blacker believes that what he has witnessed in meetings is akin to group hypnotic techniques. 'I'm not saying that there is deliberate manipulation, but people need to take account of psychological, cultural and political factors when they consider Toronto', Blacker says. Such meetings usually start with exultant worship, followed by a time of testimony about the Blessing, then more worship, and 'tips' on how to 'receive' the Blessing, then the manifestations themselves. Blacker feels that people who have a strong sense that the experience is desirable are suggestible and likely to experience it.

Despite this, he believes that 'Toronto' may be beneficial. 'If it leads to people experiencing emotional and psychological release, it will help people to become integrated, and this will lead to a spiritual freeing', he says. Many church goers have been traditionally repressed in relation to their bodies and emotions, Blacker believes, and the blessing may be a healthy, if artificial, outlet for such inhibitions. However, Blacker is concerned that the deeper psychological motivations behind the Toronto

Blessing may be less healthy. 'The effect of simulating the divine by psychological means, even if unconsciously, runs the risk of promoting a faith whose foundations are built on sand', Blacker says. 'It is an insecure faith that is drawn to experiential religion, and the problem for the church is that the truly divine may be swamped by background noise which is entirely human', he adds.

However, he has other concerns: 'Charismatic Christians often perceive themselves as an isolated and beleaguered minority, and it is quite possible that in their desire for cultural significance they rely on self-confirming supernatural manifestations to bolster a sense of corporate significance.' If the blessing is, in essence, a self-confirming confidence boost, then there is a danger that, once the impetus and intensity dies down and 'Toronto' fizzles out, this motivation could take a more damaging direction. If the Toronto Blessing reflects an insecure community in search of significance and validation, then after the 'umph' goes out of the triumph, a possible way to avoid disillusionment and doubt could be to seek to blame external factors. Blacker explains: 'The way that minority groups function is to have their group identity conferred by a shared internal experience or belief system. If this is threatened, then they achieve unity by attacking things on the outside.' This possibility becomes more credible when one considers Charismatics' aversion to doubt and questioning. 'Charismatics can be very reactionary and judgmental, and if they are psychologically tired of being disappointed, they may look for something to blame, to explain their apparent failures', Blacker says.

Philip J. Richter, a Methodist Minister and lecturer in the Sociology of Religion at the Roehampton Institute, suggests that the Toronto Blessing may reflect a sense that the novelty of the initial Charismatic manifestations has waned. The movement, he suggests, had run out of steam and the dynamic charismatic expressions had become commonplace. He sees the 'Blessing' as an attempt to satisfy the 'Charismatic marketplace': an attempt to reinvigorate, to rekindle the flames. Certainly many church leaders spoke of being at a low ebb prior to being 'Torontoed'. Indeed, Sandy Millar, vicar of Holy Trinity Brompton, has said: '(renewal) was looking very tired . . . these manifestations are restoring to us the intimacy with God for which we cried out when we first became Christians.' Richter also suggests that the leadership styles of Charismatic church leaders have become more routinized, more management orientated, as the movement has aged. Dynamic, Charismatic (in all senses) leaders had become organizers and managers; they had lost that fire in their belly for which they were once known. The readiness of many Charismatic leaders to embrace and 'teach' the Toronto Blessing, Richter says, may reflect their desire to renew the dynamic, charismatic appeal of their leadership, and to shake off routinization of their leadership styles.

The economics of religion in the marketplace is an important factor for Richter. He points out that 30,000 British pilgrims spent approximately £25 million pounds tripping to Toronto in Summer 1995. 'Experience-based religion is a highly marketable product, and the people behind the Toronto Blessing knew their market and capitalized on the consumers' demands for a thrills and spills, white-knuckle-ride religion,' he says. Richter is concerned that the 'hyping' of Toronto is exploitative, and links the marketing of Toronto with a narrowing homogenization of religious expression. 'Since it's gone global via jet-setters, the internet and publishing, it seems to me that the "Blessing" is seen as *the* legitimate expression of the Holy Spirit; in the same way that a Levi's tag is seen to authenticate jeans globally, so the "Blessing" authenticates Charismatic faith communities globally', Richter says. Toronto as a globalized, marketable commodity is unattractive to Richter, because it limits the very thing that it is supposed to offer: exploration and free expression of Christianity. It could also go out of fashion.

Dr Martyn Percy, Director of Theology and Religious Studies at Christ's College, Cambridge, describes the Toronto Blessing as 'instant mysticism'. He says, 'In the Toronto Blessing you just turn up, plug in, let go . . . and experience: easy, convenient and instant. Undoubtedly many believe this is legitimate spirituality, but I am more inclined to see it as quick, easy and consumer orientated; a sort of McDonaldization of mysticism.' When he visited Toronto he noted that the blessing was described as a 'spiritual car wash'. Percy sees it as an exchange in which participants give up their rationality in return for a warm (sometimes romantic or sexual) feeling. It costs them nothing in terms of study, work or prayer, and they receive a reassuring, affirming emotional experience.

Percy also noted the Toronto leaders' sentimental and romantic understanding of love as the ideal relationship with God. He describes the Toronto rhetoric as deeply romantic: 'Jesus sweeps you off your feet and carries you away to new heights of passion and power. The Godhead is either an indulgent father or the perfect lover anyone would willingly submit to.' In essence he sees the Toronto Blessing as a delusory, push button, feel-good factor, a sort of 'mechanistic romanticism', which, by focusing solely on the participant's personal experience, removes them from the real world.

Lloyd Pietersen, a former elder from a Charismatic church in Bristol, who is studying for a doctorate in Biblical Studies at Sheffield University, believes that despite the Toronto Blessing's apparently harmless appearance, it is a symptom of something worrying. He believes the Charismatic movement is experiencing profound disillusionment because it simply has not delivered what it promised in its infancy. Revival has not occurred (although growth has), society has not been significantly affected, let alone transformed, and the end of the world has doggedly refused to come. He points out that significant sectors of the Charismatic movement (particularly the 'new' or 'house' churches) were born in the midst of great pre-millennial fervour.

This may seem bizarre, but many Charismatics really believed (and many still do) that the movement would transform society (and the world), and that this would herald Christ's return. Even the most dynamic speakers and state of the art hype cannot convince people that the world has ended. It is fair to say that Charismatics are quick to believe things which to disinterested outsiders would seem ridiculous. Undocumented anecdotes of miracles, supernatural interventions, and dramatic skirmishes or battles in the heavenlies, are accepted with credulity and fervour in what can appear to be a desperate desire for supernatural 'proof' of their beliefs. Revival (or other signs), however, is always happening somewhere else, and is always 'just round the corner' in the UK.

Pietersen believes that because the reality does not match up to the expectation, the Charismatic community are experiencing what is known as 'cognitive dissonance'. This is best described as the discrepancy between what one believes and what one sees to be true. People generally respond to cognitive dissonance by trying to lessen it through a change of outlook, often by isolating themselves from the reality that makes the dissonance so acute. Pietersen cites the sociologist Bryan Wilson who suggested that some 'conversionist' sects respond to modern reality by an emphasis on miracles. Wilson also notes that when the millennial (end of the world) hope fades, it is replaced by an emphasis on miracles. Pietersen says: 'It seems to me that, via a process of John Wimber's teaching in the mid-eighties, the "Kansas City Prophets", and now the "Toronto Blessing", new churches have become increasingly concerned with miracles and oracles.'

The growth of spiritual warfare, personal prophecy (words of knowledge), so-called miracles and the Toronto Blessing, all bear witness to Pietersen's thesis. Pietersen believes that the Charismatic community is subconsciously highly suggestible to supernatural touches. Indeed, there is a considerable psychological imperative which makes them eager to embrace experiences which convince them of their deeply held beliefs. He suggests that these sociological and psychological forces explain the dramatic spread of the 'Toronto Blessing', and describes it as akin to stage hypnosis or religious trance-inducing rituals. In Pietersen's view, the Toronto Blessing is an expression of hopelessness and fear rather than confidence, integrity and balance. 'For all its certainty, happiness and force, it seems quite possible that, on a deeper level, it reflects insecurity, unhappiness and desperation', he says.

However, it is possible to take Pietersen's observations further, and to interpret the Toronto Blessing and other practices and trends in the Charismatic movement in a broader and more alarming way. It is clear that questions need to be asked about the movement's fascination with supernatural touches and their eagerness to engage in spiritual warfare. But it is equally clear that consideration needs to be paid to exactly where the movement is heading once the facts outface the hype and the hallelujahs dry up.

Blinded by the Light

A Cultural Context

So how are we to understand the Charismatic movement in the UK? What does it signify and where is it going? The last twenty years have seen considerable growth, and yet this does not appear to have engendered a sense of security or assurance. The last fifteen years have seen a proliferation of abusive and damaging practices. Prophecy, healing, exorcism and spiritual warfare have all caused deep and lasting harm to people with genuine faith. To many outsiders, the movement would appear to represent a frightening return to medievalism and superstition. They will say, with some reason, that this form of spirituality has nothing to offer them. Yet the rise of fundamentalism worldwide and of magical New Age beliefs in the west suggests that there are many others who are eager for spiritual certainty and 'supernatural' demonstrations of the sort that the Charismatic movement can offer. But is Christianity really to be reduced to a form of Christian magic, competing, as Elijah did with so-called false magicians to see who can make the biggest fire? Is the difference between tales of 'power healing' and New Age healing really based on a spiritual 'blood test' of the healers?

It is a truism to say that the Charismatic movement has become more experiential and this makes it likely that Charismatic theology will be simplistic – it is difficult to codify a principled, rational framework for the supernatural and magical. Martyn Percy believes that with much Charismatic theology, the tail is wagging the God: the theology follows the experiences, filling in the gaps and seeking to validate the experience. Charismatics, with their love of showy demonstration and bizarre experiences, have certainly put the 'fun' back into fundamentalism. Despite the dualistic (us and them, good and evil) approach, and the fairly rigid, personalized moral code (seen in an emphasis on family values, anti-abortion, anti-drugs and ungodly music etc.), the movement appears to reflect a wider cultural shift towards a subjective, self-orientated, experience-based approach to life.

The Charismatic movement has never been based on great principles or ethics. From the earliest days it has preferred miracles to beatitudes. It has crusaded not for issues or morals, but souls. It rarely works with or for society, but at or against it, eschewing utopia in favour of heaven or hell. But apart from the self-evident fact that it is experience based, that those social projects that it embarks on tend to have a soul-saving subtext, and that many damaging practices are associated with the movement, what are the defining characteristics of the movement and what are the consequences of these characteristics? Moreover, how does it fit into a cultural context at the end of the second millennium, and why is it experiencing rapid growth? Perhaps, most importantly, is there a healthier way for the Christianity of the twenty-first century?

Before defining the characteristics of the Charismatic movement, it is worth summarizing certain historical and cultural changes which have had an effect on the movement as it reaches the close of the millennium. Modernity refers to a worldwide movement starting in Europe in the fifteenth century, in which the world was increasingly understood from a human centred perspective. In the ancient world, the universe was viewed and understood through a theistic (God centred) matrix, but as modernity (or the Enlightenment) prevailed, via Descartes, Erasmus, Voltaire and the Reformation, man was placed at the centre of the universe, as belief in reason (rationality), science and a sense of human progress and development grew. Individualism flourished, and a secular and materialistic understanding of the human condition gained ground. The triumph of democratic capitalism is often seen as the logical outcome of modernity.

Many commentators suggest that this century has seen a shift in perspective, as humankind questions the notion of scientific (and capitalistic) rational progress. They point to the carnage of the First World War, the threat of nuclear annihilation, the breakdown of cherished institutions (the family, shared values, the church, democracy), the environmental crisis and the multiplicity of differing media voices, as leading to disillusionment with modernity. Science and reason and progress, they say, have led to the edge of the abyss, and a different paradigm, a different approach and method, is called for.

Post-modernity is the term used for the reaction against modernity. It is intrinsically suspicious of 'total' explanations, solutions or beliefs (or 'meta-narratives' – for instance, religious explanations, Marxism, scientific or humanistic progress), rejecting the concept of scientific or rational progress. Some have argued that part of the reaction against scientific modernity has been a recreation of individualistic forms of spirituality, referred to as 'remythologizing' or 're-enchantment'. Post-modernity embraces a more intuitive (sometimes seen as spiritual or even magical), ironic and tentative approach. It is uneasy with hierarchical power, and suggests that total plurality of beliefs (a centreless universe) is better, without apparently seeing that placing such a formulation on our understanding of the world is a rational act of power which some would call a meta-narrative. Nevertheless, post-modernism is more of a description than a solution.

It is into this uncertain state between modernity and post-modernity that religious movements in the west have to ply their trade. Gilles Kepel, a French academic, explains the growth of Islamic, Judaic and Christian fundamentalism as a consequence of disillusionment with modernism. According to Kepel, secular, materialistic modernity was seen not to be working. Hence, people sought certainty by reinvigorating their faith in ancient religious traditions. The breakdown and failure of modernity led them to attempt to reinvent modern society by placing an absolute religious belief at the centre. Faith had to stop adapting to and compromising with modernity; rather, modernity had to fit in with faith, hence the resurgence of fundamentalism. It is worth noting that fundamentalism, as it is broadly understood by sociologists (rather than theologians), is an absolutist historical religious belief which does not simply continue in the face of modernity (these beliefs are described as 'traditional') but *reacts against* modernity.

Dr Paul Heelas, Reader in Religion and Modernity at Lancaster University, believes that the growth of New Age beliefs also reflects tensions within modernity. People no longer have faith in the world outside, and are turning inward for a spiritual solution. Yet Heelas sees the New Age movement as a logical outcome of modernity in that its individualism has led to the New Age's primary defining characteristic: the sacralization (or making sacred) of the self. This may involve an external force or deity, but crucially, the touchstone for this relationship is the intuitive inner self. Interestingly, the New Age movement often demonstrates an emphasis on the supernatural breaking into everyday life (via healing, channelling, energies or higher consciousness), and this has clear parallels with the emphasis on divine touches in the Charismatic movement.

As we have already noted, Bryan Wilson discusses the fact that conversionist sects, when confronted with modernity, tend to rely upon miracles; and Lloyd Pietersen argues that this partially explains the emergence of the Charismatic movement and its increasing emphasis on supernatural touches. Heelas, Kepel, Wilson and others, present cogent sociological reasons for the somewhat astonishing resurgence of religious belief, and for a return to what are often perceived as superstitious and magical ancient practices. This need not undermine the validity of Charismatics' experiences, but clearly the uncertainties of modernity and the emergence of post-modernity will have shaped and informed the nature of the Charismatic movement. Culture and belief are in flux. It is an uncertain time and, as I will suggest, a critical time, for the Charismatic movement in Britain. At such a time it is pertinent to look beyond the prac-tices to the hallmarks or characteristics of the movement. The hallmarks are, for the purposes of this argument, the qualities that Charismatics themselves actually emphasize. The qualities that outsiders might wish to highlight I will examine later, as consequences of the hallmark characteristics.

Charismatic Characteristics

God-Power

An emphasis on power is one of the most obvious motifs of contemporary Charismatics. By 'power' I mean influence or force, whether in interpersonal relationships or through church struc-tures and methods of communication. This is best seen in the dogmatic hierarchical structures that many churches have. Some leaders consider themselves to be 'apostles' or 'prophets', and clearly this places them on unequal terms with their congregations. The extremes of this power imbalance are usually noted in non-denominational churches (some which practise 'shepherding'), but surely they are also prevalent in more polite form in Anglican and denominational churches. After talking to powerless women who have been ostracized after confronting leaders about sexual abuse of their colleagues these power imbalances become clear.

Less dramatically, the hierarchical structures encourage ordinary members to place their leaders on pedestals. When this pedestal appears to have a divine sanction, church members are in a powerless, sometimes dependent, position. Loyal members may speak of how 'God is *using*' leaders, but this sort of slightly awkward utterance seems to me to reflect a subconscious attempt to avoid expressing uncritical reverential adoration. Many leaders themselves use this sort of description of their ministry, and this could be interpreted as a mixture of false modesty and an embarrassment at the extent of their power and influence. Morris Cerullo regularly speaks of himself in the third person: 'Morris does not do miracles, God does miracles.'

Whether or not these leaders are protesting too much is less relevant than the fact that the onus is on them to off load their power and that they do not do so. The reality may be that with such an emphasis on power, the leaders are inextricably linked (and confused) with God. The church member's 'power relationship' with the leader resembles their relationship with God. This raises two obvious questions: what does this communicate to them about their leader, and what does it communicate to them about their God? Many have observed that Charismatic leadership often becomes domination. Church leaders do not only have opportunities to exercise (and abuse) their power in relation to prophecies, healings and exorcisms, but also in the propagation of new practices or doctrines. If concepts and practices like spiritual warfare and the Toronto Blessing had been openly debated in a disinterested, impartial fashion, it seems unlikely that they would have achieved the widespread success that they have. But articulate, powerful speakers like Gerald Coates, John Wimber, Roger Forster and countless others, enthuse about certain Charismatic practices with little apparent circumspection, and the churches accept the practices with remarkably little criticism. There is not much room for debate and, with the possible exception of the Toronto Blessing, there is almost no debate in public. Magazines like *Renewal* or *Alpha* usually toe the line of Charismatic leaders. The power of respected Charismatic leaders is such that the scandalous behaviour of the Revd Andrew Arbuthnot at the London Healing Mission was reported in the most uncritical, selective and benign manner by *Renewal* magazine. Of course, editors of such magazines are also considerable power brokers.

Further evidence of Charismatics' love of power is seen in many Charismatic publications. The number of books with the word 'power' in them is an indicator of its importance to Charismatics. John Wimber, for instance, has published *Power Evangelism*, *Power Healing*, *Power Points*, and two manuals called *Power Evangelism: Signs, Wonders and Church Growth*. There are scores of similarly titled books, choruses, tapes and features published. Whether it is power in praise, prayer or parenting, it is clear that power is a touchstone for Charismatics. Truimphalistic songs about strength, might, battle and warriors confirm this view. Power, as Wimber sees it, is proof of God, and it seems that this view is shared by the Charismatic movement. Yet is also clear that this emphasis might indeed be disempowering for everyday Christians struggling to get by. Might they not feel inadequate when confronted with examples of such unalloyed power? Might they not feel that they ought to be able to heal, prophesy, evangelize or speak in tongues with the same power as their leaders?

Moreover, is a God who uses power in these ways desirable? Dr Martyn Percy in *Words, Wonders and Power*, a study of the work and writing of John Wimber, notes: 'The power of God is often perceived as being the irresistible force meeting the moveable object.' He also notes that some of Wimber's followers believe in the possibility of God killing disobedient followers (as He is reputed to have done in the book of Acts with Ananias and Saphira). Wimber and more recent exponents of spiritual warfare clearly see life as a power battle between God and those (possibly demonic) people and forces that resist His will. The threat of God executing followers that resisted His will was quite real in the minds of the Nine O'clock Service's leaders, when Wimber was advising their abusive leader, Chris Brain. Charismatics have transformed a God who is traditionally perceived as loving, into a warlike God, a forceful dictator God. Questions need to asked about what sort of people desire a dictator and why.

The Truth, the Whole Truth

It is probably already clear that another defining characteristic of Charismatics is a belief that their view of the world is *the* view of the world: they are purveyors of The Truth. Evangelicals believed that Truth was enshrined in the innerancy of scripture, and Charismatics, in their footsteps, believe it is revealed in the innerancy of scripture *and* (Charismatic) experience. To be a practising homosexual is Wrong. To read a horoscope is Wrong. Tragic but complex issues like abortion are not discussed but pronounced on. Praising God or speaking in tongues is good, but those from other religions who do similar things are deluded and may well be engaged with the demonic. To outsiders, Charismatics may seem arrogant, dogmatic and narrow minded, but this is of no consequence: outsiders must simply realize the error of their ways.

The Good, the Bad and the Ugly

This leads on to another Charismatic hallmark: a pronounced dualism. It is not just that what they know is right, but that everything (or at least much more than in traditional Christian theology) is divided into good or evil, redeemed or fallen, Christian or demonic. At one extreme, this dualism is present in the paranoid, demon busting spiritual warfare that has spread through the movement. It is seen in the quaint but alarming rise of maverick exorcists, seeing the devil behind every ailment or problem. It is also seen in the vast market for Christian paraphernalia that has already been mentioned. There is a consciousness among Charismatics that things are contaminated if they are not Christian, and, of course, this presents a great marketing opportunity for Christian entrepreneurs. But there is a sense that exploiting this market is propagating a sort of prejudice, not dissimilar to racism. It smacks of an exclusive, defensive community, rather than an expression of what we are told is a loving God. Indeed, this dualism is also present in more progressive sectors of the movement.

For years the Evangelical Alliance appeared happy to include Morris Cerullo and others as their members, but have not joined the UK's ecumenical movement. Could it be that Cerullo is seen as a 'born again, spirit filled' Charismatic and that ecumenicalism is seen as reflecting potentially contagious liberalism. Tearfund, the relief and development agency, funded by evangelicals and Charismatics, is the UK's only major relief and development project that rarely works with the other agencies. Dewi Hughes, Tearfund's theological education adviser, has said that they work with like-minded Christians because: 'We're convinced that the essence of evangelism is the essence of the gospel, which is the essence of truth.' He points out that Tearfund knows its market and there are plenty of evagelicals who need money for development projects.

Holy Success

The emphasis on power and the exclusive dualism appear to be combined in another hallmark of the movement: an emphasis on success, albeit an alternative, Christianized form of success. What makes this success 'alternative' is not that it is significantly different from society's understanding of success, but rather, that it has a sanctifying Christian tag attached to it. In personal terms, Holy Success is seen in the accomplisment of psychological integration, health, beauty, good relationships and, sometimes, wealth. There are scores of Christian 'How To' books, covering issues such as diet, health, sex, parenting, revival, life changes, etc. The idea is that with God and the correct instructions, Christians can find fulfilment and success. With God, the story goes, we can realize our goals.

Christian magazine covers appear to mimic their worldly counterparts with images of smiling, attractive people, glossy covers, and editorial values which are a Christianized version of secular consumer-orientated magazines. The aspirational, success-orientated values and assumptions of such publications are in tune with the hedonistic, individualistic, values of secular culture. God looks after the 'King's kids' in remarkably worldly ways. This success and achievement is, in turn, seen as a reflection of being a good Christian. This theological outlook is most crudely stated in the prosperity teachings of some (but not many) Charismatic leaders. If you are following God, then He will enrich you with his abundant wealth.

Further evidence of this emphasis on Holy Success is seen in the promotion of Christian celebrities. This is interesting, because the Christian subculture has marketed and created its own celebrities (mainly rock and gospel singers) in exactly the same fashion as wider society. This imitation suggests a sneaking respect, or even awe, for the fallen 'world'. This is underlined by the Charismatic community's response when celebrities in the secular world become Christians. Minor celebrities in wider society become major celebrities on the evangelical/Charismatic circuit, eclipsing the home-grown Christian celebrities. The fact that Cliff Richard, James Fox, Paul Jones, Delia Smith, Kriss Akabusi or Jonathan Edwards are higher up in the Charismatic pecking order than home-grown celebrities, seems to testify to an awe towards the outside world. Quite what singers, actors, long jumpers, or cooks have to teach Christians is unclear; what is clear is that they left 'worldly success' for Christianity, and this appears to be the basis of their appeal. Their defection seems to give a defensive, insecure constituency a major confidence boost. It is as if they need reassuring about their faith by the presence of successes from the 'other side' who defect. They rarely hear about prominent Charismatics who 'burn out', lose their faith and defect to the world, and it is not because it does not happen.

Success for Charismatic Christians is also measured by exclusively Charismatic phenomena. Just as there may be a pressure to succeed in 'worldly' areas, so there is a pressure to succeed in the Charismatic giftings. This leads to situations in which there is an unspoken sense that to be wholly given to God one must speak in tongues, or be 'slain in the Spirit', or prophesy. This may partially explain the tremendous yearning for 'divine' touches and supernatural phenomena among Charismatics. There is, in this homogenous group, a considerable pressure to conform, and this is partly because of an idealized notion of Christian success.

As I have already hinted, this success is buoyed up and maintained by a considerable amount of optimistic and aspirational publicity material. This hype reflects a clear sense that the ends justify the means. Because they are on a mission from God, the language and techniques of the 'world' can be used without considering whether such methods treat people with respect. The medium is not the message. The message overrides every-thing. In what resembles a devastating blend of sentimentality and cynicism (surely a hallmark of contemporary 'worldly' culture), the movement shamelessly perpetuates and promotes itself to its target audience. This hype may take the form of grandiose tub-thumping exhortations of leaders, equally bombastic and unrealistic publicity materials, or a steady stream of up-beat 'encouraging' articles in magazines.

March For Jesus' ludicrous predictions-cum-prophecies, or the predictions of Dawn 2000, the Charismatic church growth organization (seven million new churches planted worldwide and 20,000 non-denominational churches in the UK by the year 2000), or the literally fantastic number of conversions predicted in missions, are good examples of hype. In 1994, the German Charismatic evangelist Reinhart Bonnke distributed a booklet to the majority of houses in Britain, and his publicity referred to millions of converts. Pentecostal churches aimed for 250,000 converts after their evangelistic 1994 'Jim' (Jesus in Me) campaign. In the event, Bonnke's campaign led to less than one convert per participating church, and evangelistic agencies involved with Jim reported 269 converts from 46 events, according to an Evangelical Alliance survey. Book titles (such as *Glasnost: Gateway to Revival* or *The Coming World Revival*) also reflect this delusory overoptimism. Charismatic Christians are perpetually encouraged to believe in revival, healings and mira-cles, and are perpetually disappointed.

I Believe

It is also clear that the Charismatic church is deeply individual-istic. It is personal conversion and personal experience of the Holy Spirit that counts. Personal spiritual development and growth are central; issues in the world outside are usually marginal. The extraordinary emphasis on worship and constant prayer are evidence of this individualized piety. The nature of the worship is interesting in itself. Charismatic choruses contain almost no theology, and largely focus on individuals feeling warm, positive, loved or cosseted. The other type of choruses are essentially war anthems against the world outside, and even these can be linked to an unhealthy individualism because, it seems, they testify to a persecuted, embattled community, and the only sense in which this can be seen as real is in their own psyches; persecution for Charismatics can be feeling that one's 'selfhood' is being challenged.

Martyn Percy points out that the revivalist movements of the past were followed by deeper social and cultural involvement, but that this is not the case with the current Charismatic movement. 'In the late modernist or post-modern revivalism, the world grows "dim" due to the personal nature of religious experience. It is the believer that becomes bathed in light; the world is left in darkness. Although Charismatics claim that the Bible is their inspiration, one has to ask where in the Bible is this obsessive personal piety, this perpetual lachrymose clamouring after Jesus' coat tails? To outsiders it seems unhealthy; to insiders it is their life source.'

Conservative Christianity

The personal nature of Charismatic religion is linked with the final hallmark of Charismatic Christianity, a deep seated conservatism. Despite the considerable work of some groups with the unemployed and underprivileged, and the experimental nature of experience-based Charismatic phenomena, the predominant thrust of the movement concerns saving souls, spiritual warfare and experiencing personal supernatural touches or blessings. Any exclusive group based upon certain dogmatic, yet traditional, key beliefs, is likely to be reactionary and defensive and a visit to a Christian bookstore confirms a deep conservatism. There are usually shelves devoted to biographies of successful Christians, personal growth, evangelism, spiritual warfare, prayer, healing, and several shelves devoted to praise and worship. Sometimes books on the 'end times' merit a shelf of their own. Little space is given to social issues. The overall impression is of a personalized, pietistic faith, and one assumes publishers know their market. When the movement works with society, the tendency is to attempt to convert, or to try to convince it of a better way. There is little sense of Charismatics entering into open dialogue or approaching outsiders with a willingness to learn or change.

The issues that they lobby for tend to be conservative. Family values, abortion, Hallowe'en, homosexual marriages and Sunday trading seem to be the issues that create the strongest reactions among Charismatics. The recent changes in divorce legislation saw the broadly based Lawyers' Christian Fellowship supporting the Lord Chancellor's removal of fault from divorce. Those in opposition were largely the evangelicals and Charismatics, in spite of reassurances from the Lawyers' Christian Fellowship that the new legislation would probably make the divorce process longer, would urge people to seek reconciliation, and would be less acrimonious and painful for couples and their children. The idea that moral fault should be dropped seemed to the Charismatics and Evangelicals to be somehow a betrayal of God.

Any attempt to distinguish characteristics of a movement is bound to involve overlap and omission. Indeed, many of the consequences of these characteristics could have been described as characteristics in their own right. However, the central hallmarks of the movement seem to me to be that it is self-evidently experiential and that there is considerable emphasis on power, absolute truth, dualism, personal piety and success, as well as an innate conservatism. The consequences of these characteristics are of more importance than the characteristics themselves.

Wedded to the World?

Some of the consequences of Charismatic practice as they affect individuals have already been described. The consequences for the movement as a whole, and how these may affect society, are addressed here. Probably the most worrying consequence of dualistic, power-orientated theology is a retreat into a 'paranoid universe' which has become a battleground for demons, malign spiritual forces, angels and the Holy Spirit. It is this which leads to 'evil' practices like 'internal ministries'; it is this which leads priests and 'counsellors' to imagine sinister Satanic machinations and to project these onto the weak and vulnerable. The Church of England is concerned at the rise of 'rogue priests' following the expansion of Charismatic belief (it is the fastest growing sector of virtually all churches in the UK); but at the less particular end of Protestantism there is less concern and greater enthusiasm for such Charismatic practices. There are few checks and balances.

The fact that prominent Anglicans like Bishop Graham Dow or Bishop David Pytches (and other bishops and senior Anglicans), and Gerald Coates and Roger Forster, the most influential New Church leaders, espouse spiritual warfare in the social and political arena, testifies to its broad appeal. It is an accepted part of Charismatic theology. Some of the claims made concerning March For Jesus in relation to spiritual warfare seem more suited to Frank Peretti's fictional *This Present Darkness* than contemporary Britain. To outsiders, the doctrine of spiritual warfare resembles a paranoid, fundamentalist retreat from reality. To insiders it is an alternative reality which the fallen ungodly 'world' cannot see. It can be seen only with spiritual lenses, by the power of the Holy Spirit.

Alongside this paranoid outlook is a simplistic understanding of society and culture (a desire for reality to be clear, certain and secure), based in the individualistic nature of Charismatic faith. There is (with notable exceptions) little desire of the Charismatic mainstream to engage with society in complex, difficult, gritty issues. As we have seen, the church is virtually silent about environmental issues, feminism and gender issues, consumerism, transport policy, unemployment or the influence of the mass media. When Charismatics do involve themselves in the world it is too often in a reactionary way, and the issues that they involve themselves in tend to be, in their eyes, clear cut. While an issue like abortion is complex (and the current laissez faire approach to it seems less than ideal), it appears that in campaigning for foetuses, they have found an innocent victim to campaign for in much the same way that vegetarians might campaign for emotionally appealing veal calves. There is a simplistic, fundamentalist fervour in both campaigns, and, in part, it seems to be sentimentally based. Violence, blasphemy or obscenity in films is another issue which evokes a simplistic response and it is these conservative causes that Charismatics tend to champion. Emotive issues and vehement simplistic reactions are traditionally the domain of adolescents. (The availability of handguns is bad, but surely a transport policy which leads to many more deaths is a more important, if difficult, cause.) Perhaps complex issues cannot be engaged by a community with a simplistic, dualistic theology. One also has to ask if it is possible for a theology that is so strongly individualized to see beyond itself?

Martyn Percy notes the shallow and simplistic nature of Charismatic theology. He says:

> There is no point in claiming healing miracles still happen today, unless you are prepared to probe why so many diseases are still with us, and then to challenge the real causes of illness, such as poverty, poor sanitation and ignorance. There is no point in a God who heals minor medical complaints in the M25 Bible Belt, but whose hands are tied when it comes to Bosnia or Burundi. Serious pain needs serious theology and *real* help.

Dietrich Bonhoeffer, the German theologian imprisoned by the Nazis and executed in 1944, made a related point concerning the state of Christianity, in one of his letters from prison, twenty years before the Charismatic movement came into existence. He explained that because of scientific and technological progress, God had been displaced from the world (in that a god-figure was no longer needed to explain or justify politics, commerce, medicine or science), and the only area that the church had any influence over was the personal and private lives of individuals. He wrote: 'As every man still has a private sphere somewhere, that is where he was thought to be most vulnerable. The secrets known to a man's valet – that is, to put it crudely, the range of his intimate life, from prayer to his sexual life – have become the hunting ground of modern pastoral workers.' He argued that the church's attempts to exploit individuals' private lives was an ignoble and un-Christian form of 'clerical trick' akin to 'religious blackmail'. A pietistic and individualistic Christian faith was, to Bonhoeffer, a sign of a defensive church with little relevance to the world.

Another cause or consequence of a simplistic and individualistic faith is an inability to mature. Paradoxically, this may also be related to Charismatics' interest in success. The marketing of spiritual success can be seen as an exploitative merry-go-round keeping Christians in an aspirational dependency which mirrors so-called worldly consumerism. Hierarchical church structures will add to this dependency. The campaigns promoting missions, miracles or new experiences (such as spiritual warfare or the Toronto Blessing) which disappoint or peter out are interesting in themselves. The fact that people respond to the publicity testifies to an extraordinary credulity in the respondents. How many times can Charismatics convince themselves that this campaign or that prophecy will really lead to revival?

Do people really believe that Morris Cerullo's 'healings' are divine, that demons evacuate areas in response to March For Jesus? The fact that people still dutifully attend suggests a desperation in their believing. All the evidence suggests that revival simply is not going to happen (their methods and 'God's' words have patently failed to deliver), yet almost perversely, they hope against hope. Lloyd Pietersen has suggested that Charismatics have an inability to learn because of the effect of continual hype. He believes that Charismatics are wary of examining their failures, because this may cause them to ask questions which will shake the foundations of their faith. This stops them maturing because they are damned to a perpetual pre-occupation with the cusp of the new. The stupendous credulity among Charismatic Christians as they swallow cartoon-book miracles or divine interventions maintains a brittle optimism while making maturity impossible.

However, because their power and success-orientated 'gospel' is forced to overreach itself, in the long term the difference between theory and practice will become clear. Fifty per cent of the cancer sufferers that Wimber prays for are not going to be healed. Revival is not coming home. What new experiences can the movement (unconsciously) generate after the Toronto Blessing? It is quite possible that the Toronto Blessing is a desperate cry, a last gasp attempt at self-validation. Yet it is difficult to see how the movement can come up with anything more experiential and more exotic. The psychiatrist Russell Blacker has pointed out that once the theories, beliefs and experiences of a minority group become threatened, there is a tendency to unite against a hostile world.

Predictions, like prophecies, are hostages to fortune. Yet it seems quite possible that the Charismatic movement could start looking for scapegoats to blame for its apparent failures. Spiritual warfare has been described as a spiritual scapegoating. Charismatics had been so full of expectation of signs and wonders and revival that when, once again, it failed to materialize, they needed some explanation of this. The doctrine of spiritual warfare provided this because it suggested that before God could work, opposing spiritual powers needed to be vanquished. The aggressive, combative tone of the language of spiritual warfare has been described as 'spiritual violence' and is evidence of a community spoiling for a fight. It is as if all their disappointment and righteous indignation was channelled into this wrathful phenomenon.

However, scapegoating in the physical realm is a more worrying phenomenon. The church's conservative agenda suggests a number of minorities that would fit the bill as scapegoats. Homosexuals seem an obvious target for a number of reasons. The gay 'problem' is clearly the next big issue for the Church of England and it is already apparent that homophobia is going to be more difficult to overcome than the fear of women being priests. In non-denominational Charismatic churches, equal rights for gays are simply not on the agenda. New Agers, Wiccans, and other religious minorities present another possibility for scapegoating. In the USA, the rhetoric of the Taxpayers' political party and of others on the fundamentalist right, that doctors who do abortions should face the death penalty and homosexuals be killed, provide a chilling precedent.

If scapegoating were to occur it would present the movement with a watershed moment, because while some might participate and others stand by without approving, there would be others in the Charismatic movement who could not countenance such a phenomenon. It may well lead them to ask some hard questions and make some hard decisions concerning their faith. If the more progressive minority were to leave the mainstream (and there are signs of this already), the mainstream would, of course, become more extreme.

I will examine the 'fallout' from the Charismatic movement in the next chapter, but a related issue is the preponderance of fragmentation (or schism) in the movement. Many have observed that the Charismatic movement is prone to division. Martyn Percy believes that this fragmentation is primarily because the Charismatic movement is based on feeling rather than theology. He says, 'Their theology, if you can call it that, is done through the hormones and not in the head. Experience always precedes reflection.' It is because the movement is based on what Percy calls a 'community of feeling', rather than a theology, that the possibility of fragmentation increases. Because the community values experience rather than reason, there is an intellectual vacuum that powerful charismatic leaders can exploit with powerful experiences. The more charismatic (in both senses) the leader, and the more powerful the experiences that he is offering, the more likely he is to gain a following and possibly cause a split. Hence, Percy explains, Charismatic groups are 'always open to the ravages of subjective individualism'. He says, 'Without an adequate theology, the movement will continue to fragment at the same rate at which it grows.' Such fragmentation could prove dangerous with maverick leaders, particularly if groups are defensive towards outside culture. Surely this is what happened to Christian-based communities in Jonestown and Waco.

Charismatics, Modernity and the New Age

If scapegoating and fragmentation are likely consequences of Charismatic belief, it is worth considering the movement in relation to modernity (or what they would call the 'world') and in relation to their spiritual competitors, the New Age movement. Are they really as different as Charismatics would have us believe? One of the favourite phrases of Charismatics concerns their relationship to the 'world'. It is a paraphrase of some verses in the second letter to the Corinthians and is an exhortation that Christians should 'be in the world but not of the world'. It is usually taken to mean that Christians should be involved in the world but with an 'alternative' value system and motivation. It is my view that the exact opposite is a more accurate reflection of the Charismatic movement at present. It appears that, as people take an increasingly fervent approach to Charismatic experiences and develop a paranoid world view based on an extreme view of demonology, they are rapidly retreating from the world. Given this and their traditional separation from the world, one has to ask how they can judge whether or not they are 'of' the world. Their lack of understanding of the world has led to a superficial interpretation of the nature of worldliness, which is frequently linked with smoking, drinking, swearing, listening to rock music and other surface cultural features. If worldliness is taken to mean being like the world, or modernity, it seems that the Charismatic movement is *deeply* worldly, for a number of reasons.

I have already suggested that an innate conservatism and an emphasis on power and success are key characteristics of the Charismatic movement, and it is obvious that these reflect contemporary society. Indeed modernity, particularly in the USA, appears almost enslaved to these values and attitudes. Wealth, success, status, beauty and a fairly brazen fascination with that multi-faceted catch-all, power, are the driving forces behind capitalist modernity. The individualistic nature of this widespread promotion of rational self-interest and pleasure seeking, is also reflected in the church and the individualized experiences that it emphasizes. In addition, the 'prayer hotlines', the Christian satellite channels, and the fundamentalist web sites testify (among other things) to the tools of modernity serving individuals' religious needs. The 'How to' books testify to a culture based upon achievement and performance. This is not to say that the church fails to act as a supportive and warm community to its members, but beyond this, there is a growing emphasis on the personalized and the pietistic within the movement. It should also be noted that the church's exclusive nature reflects an increasingly fragmented, atomized society, made up of different and distinct interest groups fighting their respective corners. It is a little like a single issue political party or lobby, and the issue is: are you saved/spirit filled/anointed?

The Charismatic movement's marketing and promotion also reflects an uncritical use of modernity's tools to exploit the 'market'. The continual use of hype to promote the *new* experience, church growth technique, preacher or campaign is a mirror image of 'worldly' consumerism. I imagine that there are sociologists and cultural commentators who have examined the emphasis of Charismatic fundamentalists on the distinctive, dogmatic be born again, spirit-filled message (as opposed to their methods, principles and values) as an aspect of modernity. The fact the Charismatics believe that the distinctive nature of their message makes them unworldly certainly appears to reflect a shallow, consumer-orientated outlook.

Is a Charismatic Christian's alleged healing or prophetic insight substantially or qualitatively different from a New Ager's? Is Charismatic Christianity merely a spiritual designer label? Indeed, if the message is the only distinctive feature which draws a line between the church and the world, what is left of the message? A belief system or message with no outward consequences is merely a religious tag. The methods, attitudes, goals and values are indistinguishable from society's, so the church is tailor made for society. Therefore it cannot challenge society. If the Christian message is to transform individuals and society, the Charismatic incarnation of the message can have little effect. It can only attract those that are deeply imbued with modernity's values and who want a bolt-on spiritual dimension. It can, thus, only become confirmed in its fundamentalist conservatism.

However, surprisingly, the Charismatic movement also reflects much within the New Age movement, its sworn enemy. Dr Paul Heelas has explored the extent to which the New Age movement is an aspect of modernity, and his analysis offers interesting insights into Charismatic Christianity. One of Heelas' key points about the New Age is that it is an amorphous group of belief systems which unite in rejecting externally imposed dogmatic beliefs in favour of internal, subjective spirituality based in the inner self. Clearly New Agers and Charismatics differ considerably in their approach to dogma (though it could be pointed out that some New Age groups have dogmas of their own). They have more in common, however, in their emphasis on the self. The increasingly individualized, experiential nature of Charismatic practice places the 'self' as an entity at the heart of the theology. Heelas links this emphasis in the New Age with the emergence and influence of psychology and psychiatry in the modern world, and sees the New Age's making the self sacred as a natural extension of this cultural trajectory. Although Charismatics believe in dogmatic, external reality, the centrality of the self to their theology and practice probably has similar roots.

The belief in the efficacy of this inner spirituality is present in both movements, and, on occasions, in some strikingly similar manifestations. Both groups are keen to experience supernatural touches (whether from the Holy Spirit or from the energies, or forces that underpin the universe), and both appear to show a remarkable credulity when offered healers and miracle workers. There is a ferocious fascination with magic in both camps. The doctrine of spiritual warfare, which suggested that a certain number of worshipping Christians around the global timezones would vanquish the demonic and herald world revival, has marked similarities with the beliefs of Maharishi Mahesh Yogi's Transcendental Meditation (and many others). These state that once a certain proportion of the population meditates, then the harmonic energies that are released will lower crime rates, road accidents and mental illness, and usher in a better age. Another interesting comparison is between New Age visualization, in which participants concentrate on what they desire in the belief that this will make it happen, and the prosperity teaching (sometimes called 'name it and claim it') of some Charismatics, which posits that Christians must pray for things and expect to receive them. Both Charismatics and New Agers offer simplistic, quick fix solutions, which are based in magic and superstition, to social and personal problems.

Another interesting comparison between Charismatics and

New Agers is a pronounced dualism. Significant sectors (although not all) of the New Age see themselves as offering an alternative to modernity; life is divided up between the natural and holistic, and the artificial and mechanistic. This division appears to have more integrity than the 'us and them, saved and unsaved' dualism of the Charismatic movement, in that it is attempting to challenge society, although it also sees society as a threat and in need of enlightenment or salvation.

Yet this difference is worthy of discussion. New Agers are more inclusive and deeply suspicious of dogma, whereas Charismatics are exclusive and committed to dogma. New Age belief is much broader and there is evidence that it attracts educated liberals, whereas the Charismatic movement tends to attract conservatives. It has been argued that the radical subjectivity of the New Age can lead to radical abuse because there is a belief vacuum in which anything can occur. The Charismatic movement, on the other hand, has to face the possibility of radical dogmatism leading to radical abuse. This is particularly likely because the constituency has a heritage of belief in dogma (which in relation to Christian principles might be seen as offering some protection), which is reflected in dogmatic leaders and hierarchical leadership structures. Yet at the same time as preaching within a dogmatic tradition, many of the teachers are espousing much more subjective, experiential doctrines and practices. New Agers could respond to such teachings by rejecting them on the basis that they did not resonate with their 'inner selves', but Charismatics are not primed for such a response. They are more open to abuse because Christian ethics or doctrines have given way to Christian experience *and* because they are used to not questioning authority. They mistakenly see what they are being taught as based in historical doctrine, but, in reality, it owes more to a tradition of dogmatic leadership.

The potential for abuse within the Charismatic movement is massive. The characteristics of the movement merit one last comparison. Dr Eileen Barker, a sociologist at the London School of Economics, who specializes in studying new religious movements (popularly known as cults), describes a number of potentially dangerous situations in which members may find themselves. In her book, *New Religious Movements*, she writes:

Among the *potentially* dangerous situations to which the reader has been alerted are:

- A movement cutting itself off (either geographically or socially) from the rest of society.
- A convert becoming increasingly dependent on the movement for definitions and the testing of 'reality.'
- A movement drawing sharp, unnegotiable boundaries between 'them' and 'us', 'godly' and 'satanic', 'good' and 'bad' – and so on.
- Important decisions about converts' lives being made for them by others.
- Leaders claiming divine authority for their actions and demands.
- Leaders or movements pursuing a single goal in a single-minded manner.

I need not press the point home.

In Our End Is Our Beginning?

The rather gloomy prognosis that this book offers for the Charismatic Church flies in the face of one particularly pertinent fact. The Charismatic Church is in the ascendant. Worldwide, some estimates suggest that there are as many as 400 million Charismatic Christians, and many point to quite phenomenal growth, particularly in developing countries. The movement has come from nothing into a major Christian force, and some commentators estimate that Charismatics now represent 20 per cent of the world's Christian population. In the UK there are Charismatics in virtually all denominations, and again, estimates of numbers vary between several hundred thousand and over a million. It is indisputably the fastest growing church in the UK and worldwide. Critics (and I include myself) see this as alarming. I have suggested a number of reasons why the Charismatic Church might appeal to modern culture. In so far as it shares modern society's methods and values, it is an easy religion for conservative minded people to attach themselves to. It offers a relatively costless spirituality (or, as Bonhoeffer would have put it, a form of 'cheap grace'). Yet it is also clear that the majority culture will view its exotic practices and rigid dogma as fundamentalist and reactionary. Modernity has not accommodated itself to Charismatics; the accommodation is entirely on the part of the church.

I have described the 'fallout' from the Charismatic Church in terms of individuals' stories. However, there is another sort of fallout which may be viewed more positively. In his book *The Post-Evangelical*, Dave Tomlinson describes having had scores of encounters with disaffected Charismatics who felt ready to give up on Christianity. It is a book which charts a theological and spiritual escape route for Charismatics and evangelicals who simply could not ignore the tensions and dissatisfactions within their faith, and it clearly struck a nerve. Tomlinson has had hundreds of letters from people who were on a similar pilgrimage. He says: 'I was overwhelmed by the letters which I received from strikingly different people; they were generally fed up with the narrowness and dogmatic nature of their faith, but wanted to maintain a faith which was not theologically liberal; they wanted a real belief in God.' These people had experienced what they considered to be an authentic experience of Christ, but they found attendance at Charismatic or evangelical churches increasingly difficult.

Another indicator of increasing disaffection with the Charismatic mainstream is the number of people starting experimental 'alternative worship' churches. These are services (or churches) which grew out of dissatisfaction with conventional Charismatic worship. It was not just that they found the saccharine, guitar-strumming choruses to be very bad music, but that it was culturally alien to them. People felt that they wanted to worship using music and imagery which had some cultural resonance for them. The culture of the Charismatic Church appeared to have turned God into the equivalent of a Radio Two presenter on Prozac. It was bland and syrupy, but with a manic and dogmatic subtext.

Yet it was more than simply differences in taste that led to the growth of alternative worship groups or alternative churches. There was a strong reaction against the churches' dogmatic attitudes, and a feeling that they were silent on issues that mattered – gender issues, the environment, racism, creating community and wealth distribution. These people reacted against the Charismatic emphasis on power, success, absolute truth and the reactionary paranoid dualism that seemed to infuse the movement. They were interested in shared leadership, in experimenting with forms of community (often the 'churches' were simply informal meetings of like minded people in night clubs, pubs or houses), and with learning from other faiths and cultures while maintaining a Christian faith. It did not seem just that non-Christians were bound for hell, or that homosexuals could not consummate their relationships. They wanted to hold on to a relationship with Christ, but felt that they could not put Christian dogma before people. They were not willing to allow things to be as black and white as they had been told. Whereas the Charismatic movement is deeply conservative, these people would tend to be much more liberal in their outlook.

Chris Brain and the Nine O'clock Service were at the cutting edge of this movement, particularly when they started to criticize the Charismatic fundamentalism that had brought them into being. One of their fliers stated that they were 'moving away from unhealthy models for religion that make people dependent. Rigid dogma, abusive power structures, clericalism and cults of personality all seem to be dependent and contribute to a disempowering condition called religious codependence.' Despite the fact that these radical aims were masking exactly the sorts of abuses that they were highlighting, they epitomized the agenda of many of the UK's two hundred alternative churches.

Tomlinson refers to those involved with the 'alternative church' as post-evangelicals (taken to include Charismatics), and suggests that they reflect a wider cultural shift from a rational, modernistic outlook to a more holistic, post-modern approach. He says:

> My thesis is simple: that post-evangelicals tend to be people who identify culturally more with the more tentative post-modernity (the culture of the post-modern) than with modernity; their belief combines faith and doubt, commitment and enquiry, confession and self-criticism; the faith of evangelicals and Charismatics tends to be total, and replete with pseudo-rational laws which in fact owe more to modernity than to Christianity.

He adds, 'It is ironic that the fundamentalist, Charismatic church which is clearly deeply superstitious and irrational, tries to use rationality to convince people of its relevance. Its emphasis on magic and the supernatural can be seen as post-modern in that it is a reaction against scientific materialism but it is also deeply rooted in modernity.' He sees it is a perplexing and apparently immiscible cocktail, but one which, despite its magical aspect, is fundamentally modernist. Another irony is that post-evangelicals, who are deeply suspicious of the dogmatic approach of Charismatics, are using ritual and imagery that draw on ancient church practice. If Tomlinson is right, then the breakaway alternative church movement differs from the Charismatic movement in ways which suggest that it may have more to offer the evolving post-modern culture than the Charismatic church. It is impossible to know what the 'alternative church' offers British Christianity in the long term, but its members have inherited the drive of Charismatics, albeit in a much more self-critical, questioning and tentative way.

Grace Davie, a Sociology lecturer at Exeter University, in her book *Religion in Britain since 1945: Believing Without Belonging,* supports the idea that contemporary Christians are disillusioned with church membership. The vast majority of people in Britain claim to have religious beliefs but are not members of religious institutions. For most, she says, this is simply a 'fall-back position', because they are not motivated to act and make decisions about religious issues, but rest on the tacit religious beliefs that they have inherited. Davie points out that these people are likely to be open to diverse religious beliefs, including New Age beliefs, and likens this to post-modern 'pick and mix' individualized religious behaviour. However, she also recognizes the reaction of conservative religious expression against this individualistic fragmentation, in the rise of fundamentalism.

The alternative, or post-evangelical, church appears to have a foot in both camps – although in no sense is its Christianity fundamentalist. Its essential beliefs are Christian, yet it is reacting against much that is considered religious. It is also much more open to 'the world outside', including other religions and older Christian traditions. Davie notes that those influenced by post-modernity tend to have 'a space for the sacred but often in forms different from those which have gone before'. Clearly this is true for alternative church groups (as well as New Agers) in their more meditative, image-, music- and ritual-based approach to worship. Interestingly, because of much looser organizational structures, the alternative church also offers people the opportunity to believe without belonging, and possibly this will make it attractive to people disinclined to subscribe to either eclectic New Age beliefs, or dogmatic traditional or Charismatic beliefs. Much will depend on how these churches utilize their critiques of hierarchy and power as they become institutionalized over time. Radical power sharing is hard to sustain, particularly as numbers increase.

Strangely, one theologian whose attacks on the church are reminiscent of the post-evangelicals' attacks on the Charismatic

Church, and who seems to have much in common with the alternative church, was executed before the Charismatic Church existed. Dietrich Bonhoeffer was an evangelical pastor and theologian in wartime Germany, who initially was a pacifist, highly critical of the Nazis, but who was later imprisoned and hanged for his involvement in an attempt to assassinate Hitler. Bonhoeffer's early writings emphasized finding Christ in Christian community and what he called 'cheap grace', which was the sort of religious belief which demanded little of the believer (I have already referred to this in relation to the experiential power- and success-orientated Charismatic movement). It was in the last months of Bonhoeffer's life in prison that his theology became truly radical. In his letters to Eberhard Bethge, a friend and fellow pastor, he wrote of the 'world coming of age' and of shoddy 'clerical tricks' which the church used to maintain its waning dominion or influence over people. He argued that God as a concept was no longer needed for contemporary man, because of the discoveries of science, and progress in ethics, politics and the arts. The Enlightenment, which led towards human autonomy, had reached such a degree of completion that God was redundant. He called this situation 'the coming of age' of humanity, and believed that God was being displaced and pushed out of life by humanistic progress. He asked: 'If our final judgement must be that the western form of Christianity was only a preliminary stage to a complete absence of religion, what kind of situation emerges for us, for the church?'

However, he saw this 'displacement of God from the world' as positive, and was critical of the church's last-ditch rearguard action of attempting to reassert its dominion in relation to human beings' areas of vulnerability – their inner lives, secret sins and awareness of death. He likened this emphasis on human weaknesses to the activities of gutter journalists, and considered it ignoble and un-Christian to home in on people in their areas or moments of weakness. He wrote: 'So our coming of age leads us to a true recognition of our situation before God. God would have us know that we must live as men who manage our lives without him.' Bonhoeffer saw this as a form of emancipation which must be viewed positively, and this led to a radical reinterpretation of the Christian message. 'The God who lets us live in the world without the working hypothesis of God is the God before whom we stand continually. Before God and with God we live without God. God lets himself be pushed out of the world on to the cross. He is weak and powerless in the world, and that is precisely the way, the only way, in which he is with us and helps us', he wrote. He argued that God helps people not by his power, but by his suffering and weakness, and that this is the crucial difference between Christianity and other religions. Christianity, he thought, should not be a religion of power but of powerlessness.

Bonhoeffer suggested that the essence of what was wrong with historical Christianity was its emphasis on God's omnipotence and power, and he predicted that in the future people would distrust this. He rejected religion because it was a self-serving power structure, and suggested that Christians should live without 'false religious obligations and inhibitions'. He wrote:

> To be a Christian does not mean to be religious in a particular way, to make something of oneself (a sinner, a penitent or a saint) on the basis of some method or other, but to be a man – not a type of man, but the man that Christ makes in us. It is not the religious act that makes a Christian, but participation in the sufferings of God in the secular life.

Bonhoeffer's vision of Christianity was the opposite of the paranoid dualism of today's Charismatic church. Equally important, his approach to power is in opposition to the approach of modern Charismatics. He wrote to Bethge explaining that he learnt to have faith by 'living unreservedly in life's duties, problems, successes and failures, experiences and perplexities. In so doing we throw ourselves completely into the arms of God, taking seriously, not our own sufferings, but those of God in the world.' In an outline of a book that he planned to write, Bonhoeffer wrote:

> The church is only the church when it exists for others. To make a start, it should give away all its property to those in need. The clergy must live solely on the freewill offerings of their congregations, or possibly engage in some worldly calling. The church

must share in the secular problems of ordinary human social life, not dominating, but helping and serving. It must tell men of every calling what it means to live with Christ, to live for others. In particular, our own church will have to take the field against the vices of hubris, power-worship, envy and illusion, as the roots of all evil. It will have to speak of moderation, authenticity, trust, loyalty, constancy, patience, discipline, humility, contentment and modesty.

Whether or not the Charismatic Church's 'bastard child', the alternative church, will live up to this remains to be seen. But surely Bonhoeffer's vision of Christianity has much to offer the church of the next century. In a religion so deeply rooted in vulnerability and sacrifice, it is surprising that it has become so reactionary, so keen on domination and power. The Christ one reads of in the New Testament deserves a more generous interpretation. The Incarnation, one assumes, was a supreme symbol of vulnerability and empathy. Equally one might expect Christians to interpret the Cross as a demonstration of weakness and selfless love. Rather than seeing the Resurrection as an act of ultimate triumph and victory, it is better understood as a testament to a deeper truth and a better way, to values that are not extinguished by death. It seems to me that it is only when Christianity becomes synonymous with selflessness that it can have a radical future, and a future which offers hope and a universal challenge to individuals and society. Only then may the church become the Bride of Christ.

Bibliography

Barker, E., *New Religious Movements*, 1989, HMSO.

Bethge, E., *Bonhoeffer*, 1979, Fount.

Bonhoeffer, D., *Letters and Papers From Prison*, 1971, SCM.

Bruce, S., *Pray TV*, 1990, Routledge.

Cotton, I., *The Hallelujah Revolution*, 1995, Little, Brown & Co.

Davie, G., *Religion in Britain Since 1945*, 1995, Blackwells.

Dow, G., *Explaining Deliverance*, 1991, Sovereign World.

Fearon, M., *A Breath of Fresh Air*, 1994, Eagle.

Hocken, P., *Streams of Renewal*, 1986, Paternoster.

Horrobin, P., *Healing Through Deliverance*, 1991, Sovereign World.

Heelas, P., *The New Age Movement*, 1996, Blackwell.

Kraft, C. H., *Defeating Dark Angels*, 1993, Sovereign World.

Kendrick, G., Coates, G., Forster, R. and Green, L., *March For Jesus*, 1992, Kingsway.

Percy, M., *Words, Wonders and Power*, 1996, SPCK.

Peretti, F., *This Present Darkness*, 1986, Crossway Books.

Prince, D., *Spiritual Warfare*, 1987, Whitaker House.

Porter, S. and Richter, P., *The Toronto Blessing*, 1995, Darton, Longman & Todd.

Rees-Larcombe, J., *Unexpected Healing*, 1991, Hodder & Stoughton.

Scotland, N., *Charismatics and the Next Millennium*, 1995, Hodder & Stoughton.

Smail, T., Walker, A. and Wright, N., *Charismatic Renewal*, 1993, SPCK.

Subritsky, B., *Demons Defeated*, 1986, Sovereign World.

Storm, R., *Exorcists*, 1993, Fount.

Tomlinson, D., *The Post-Evangelical*, 1995, Triangle.

Wagner, P., *Warfare Prayer*, 1992, Monarch.

Walker, A., *Restoring the Kingdom*, 1985, SPCK.

White, J., *When the Spirit Comes With Power*, 1989, Hodder & Stoughton.

Wimber, J., *Power Evangelism*, 1985, Hodder & Stoughton.

Wimber, J., *Power Healing*, 1986, Hodder & Stoughton.

Wimber, J., *Healing Seminar*, 1985, Vineyard.